SAS Publishing

Data Mining Using Enterprise Miner™ Software: A Case Study Approach

First Edition

The Power to Know™

57872

Table of Contents

Overview

This book covers the basic skills that are required to assemble and understand some basic data mining analyses with the Enterprise Miner tool set.

To learn more...

A full curriculum of general and statistical instructor-based training is available at any of the Institute's training facilities. Institute instructors can also provide on-site training.

For information about other courses in the curriculum, contact the Education Division at 1-919-677-8000, then press 1-7321, or send e-mail to saspsd@vm.sas.com. You can also find this information on the Web at www.sas.com/training/ as well as in the Training Course Catalog.

For a list of other SAS books that relate to the topics that are covered here, U.S. customers can contact our Fulfillment Services Department at 1-800-727-3228 or send e-mail to sasbook@sas.com. Customers outside the USA should contact their local SAS office.

See the Publications Catalog on the Web at www.sas.com/pubs for a complete list of books and a convenient order form.

Prerequisites

Before using this book, you should be familiar with Microsoft Windows and software that is based on Windows.

General Conventions

This section explains the various conventions that are used in presenting text, SAS language syntax, and examples in this book.

Typographical Conventions

This book uses several type styles. This list displays the meaning of each style:

UPPERCASE ROMAN	is used for SAS statements, variable names, and other SAS language elements when they appear in the text.
italic	identifies terms or concepts that are defined in text. Italic is also used for book titles when they are referenced in text, as well as for various syntax and mathematical elements.
bold	is used for emphasis within text, and to indicate selectable items in windows and menus. This book also uses icons to represent selectable items.
`monospace`	is used for examples of SAS programming statements and for SAS character strings. Monospace is also used to refer to field names in windows, information in fields, and user-supplied information.

Note: In general, tabs and menu headings do not appear in a different font. These headings appear in bold if you are being requested to click on the heading. Otherwise, the heading title is capitalized.

Mouse Conventions

The number of buttons on mouse devices varies. On mouse devices with two or three buttons, one button makes selections and one button displays pop-up menus. The locations of these buttons depend on the mouse settings. In the default configuration, the left mouse button is the select button and the right mouse button displays the menu as shown below. Identify the buttons on your mouse that correspond to the select button and the menu button respectively. Note: This book uses the verbs *click* to indicate clicking on the select button and *right-click* to indicate clicking on the menu button. In addition, the book uses the verb *select* to indicate clicking on the select button.

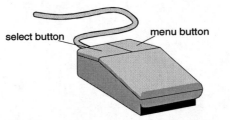

Two-Button Mouse with Default Settings

Chapter 1: Introduction

1.1 Getting Started

Opening Enterprise Miner

To start Enterprise Miner, double-click on the Enterprise Miner icon on your desktop. If no icon is available and you are running on Windows, use the Start menu and select **Start → Programs → Enterprise Miner → Enterprise Miner X.x,** where *X.x* represents the version number of Enterprise Miner that you have installed on your machine.

Setting Up the Initial Project and Diagram

Enterprise Miner organizes analyses into projects and diagrams. Each project may have several diagrams, and each diagram may contain several analyses. Typically each diagram contains an analysis of one data set.

1. Select **File → New → Project**.
2. Type in the name of the project (for example, `My Project`).
3. Check the box for **Client/server project** if necessary.
   Note: You must have the access to a server that runs the same version of Enterprise Miner. See *Getting Started with the Enterprise Miner* or the online help if you want to build a client/server project.

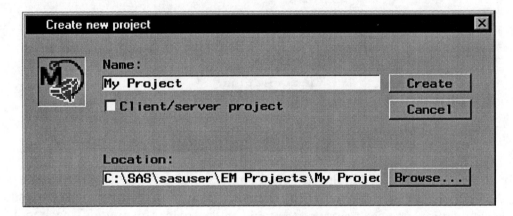

4. Modify the location of the project folder if you want by selecting **Browse**.
5. Select **Create**. The project opens with an initial untitled diagram.

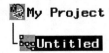

6. Click on the diagram title and type in a new title (for example, My First Flow).

After Selecting Name	**Final Appearance**
▓My Project	▓My Project
└▓Untitled	└▓My First Flow

Identifying the Workspace Components

7. Observe that the project window opens with the Diagrams tab activated. Select the **Tools** tab that is located to the right of the Diagrams tab in the lower-left portion of the project window. This tab enables you to see all of the tools (or nodes) that are available in Enterprise Miner.

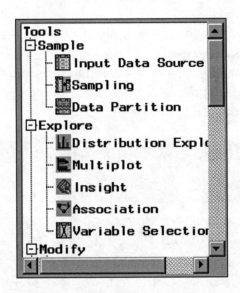

Many of the commonly used tools are shown on the toolbar at the top of the window. You can add additional tools to this toolbar by dragging them from the window above onto the toolbar. In addition, you can rearrange the tools on the toolbar by dragging each tool to a new location on the bar.

8. Select the **Reports** tab that is located to the right of the Tools tab. This tab displays any reports that have been generated for this project. This is a new project, so no reports are currently available.

9. Return to the Tools tab.

1.2 Data Mining Using SEMMA

Definition of Data Mining

There are many techniques that can be grouped under the name *Data Mining*. SAS Institute defines data mining as "advanced methods for exploring and modeling relationships in large amounts of data."

Overview of the Data

The data often comes from several different sources, and combining information from these different sources may present quite a challenge. The need for better and quicker access to information has generated a great deal of interest in building Data Warehouses that are able to quickly assemble and deliver the needed information in usable form. A typical data set has many thousand observations. An observation may represent an individual customer, a specific transaction, or a certain household. The data set also contains specific information (or variables) about each observation such as demographic information, sales history, or financial information. How this information is used depends on the research question of interest.

When talking about types of data, it is important to consider the *measurement level* of each variable. You can generally classify each variable into one of the following categories:
- *interval* - a variable for which the mean (or average) makes sense, such as average income or average temperature.
- *categorical* - a variable consisting of a set of levels, such as gender (male or female) or drink size (small, regular, large). In general, if the variable is not continuous (taking the average does not make sense, such as *average gender*), then it is categorical. Categorical data can be split up in several ways. For the purposes of Enterprise Miner, consider these subgroupings of categorical variables:
  - *unary* - a variable that has the same value for every observation in the data set.
  - *binary* - a variable that has only two possible levels (i.e. gender).
  - *nominal* - a variable that has more than two levels, but the ordering of the levels has no implied order (i.e., pie flavors - cherry, apple, and peach).
  - *ordinal* - a variable that has more than two levels, and the ordering of the levels has an implied order (i.e., drink size - small, regular, large). Note: Ordinal variables may be treated as nominal variables (i.e., if you are not interested in the ordering of the levels), but nominal variables cannot be treated as ordinal variables since there is no implied ordering by definition.

To obtain a meaningful analysis, you must construct an appropriate data set and specify the correct measurement level for each of the variables.

Overview of the Methods

Predictive Modeling Techniques enable the analyst to identify whether a set of input variables is useful in predicting some outcome variable. For example, a financial institution may try to determine if knowledge of an applicant's income and credit history (input variables) helps to predict whether the client is likely to default on a loan (outcome variable).

To distinguish the input variables from the outcome variables, set the *model role* for each variable in the data set. Identify outcome variables by using the *target* model role, and identify input variables by using the *input* model role. If you wish to exclude some of the variables from the analysis, identify these variables by using the *rejected* model role. Specify a variable as an ID variable by using the *ID* model role.

Predictive modeling techniques require one or more outcome variables of interest. Each technique attempts to predict the outcome as well as possible according to some criteria such as *maximizing accuracy* or *maximizing profit*. This book shows you how to use several predictive modeling techniques by using Enterprise Miner including *Regression Models*, *Decision Trees*, and *Neural Networks*. Each of these techniques enables you to predict a binary, nominal, or continuous outcome variable from any combination of input variables. Decision Trees and Neural Networks can also model ordinal targets.

Descriptive Techniques enable the analyst to identify underlying patterns in a data set. These techniques do not have a specific outcome variable of interest. This book explores how to use Enterprise Miner to perform the following descriptive techniques:
- *Cluster analysis*: This analysis attempts to find natural groupings of observations in the data, based on a set of input variables. After grouping the observations into clusters, the analyst can use the input variables to try to characterize each group. Once the clusters have been identified and interpreted, the analyst may decide to treat each cluster independently.
- *Association analysis*: This analysis identifies groupings of products or services that tend to be purchased at the same time or at different times by the same customer. The analysis would answer questions such as
  - What proportion of the people who purchased eggs and milk also purchased bread?
  - What proportion of the people who have a car loan with some financial institution later obtain a home mortgage from the same institution?

Understanding SEMMA

The tools are arranged according the SAS process for Data Mining, SEMMA.

SEMMA stands for

Sample - identify input data sets (identify input data; sample from a larger data set; partition data set into training, validation, and test data sets).

Explore - explore data set statistically and graphically (plot the data, obtain descriptive statistics, identify important variables, perform association analysis).

Modify - prepare the data for analysis (create additional variables or transform existing variables for analysis, identify outliers, replace missing values, modify the way in which variables are used for the analysis, perform cluster analysis, analyze data with self-organizing maps (known as SOMs) or Kohonen networks).

Model - fit a predictive model (model a target variable by using a regression model, a decision tree, a neural network, or a user-defined model).

Assess - compare competing predictive models (build charts that plot percentage of respondents, percentage of respondents captured, lift, and profit).

The Score node is grouped with the tools under **A**ssess and is designed to capture scoring code for the models that have been fit. The scoring code can be saved as a SAS program outside Enterprise Miner. The SAS program can then be run on any platform that runs base SAS. Thus, you can perform the actual scoring on almost any type of platform.

Additional tools are available under the Utility nodes group.

Overview of the Nodes

Sample Nodes

The Input Data Source node reads data sources and defines their attributes for later processing by Enterprise Miner. This node can perform various tasks:
1. It enables you to access SAS data sets and data marts. Data marts can be defined by using the SAS Data Warehouse Administrator, and they can be set up for Enterprise Miner by using the Enterprise Miner Warehouse Add-ins.
2. It automatically creates a metadata sample for each variable when you import a data set with the Input Data Source node. By default, Enterprise Miner obtains the metadata sample by taking a random sample of 2,000 observations from the data set that is identified in the Input Data Source. Optionally, you can request larger samples. If the data is smaller than 2,000 observations, the entire data set is used.
3. It uses the metadata sample to set initial values for the measurement level and the model role for each variable. You can change these values if you are not satisfied with the automatic selections that are made by the node.
4. It displays summary statistics for interval and class variables.
5. It enables you to define target profiles for each target in the input data set.

Note: For the purposes of this document, **data sets** and **data tables** are equivalent terms.

The Sampling node enables you to perform random sampling, stratified random sampling, and cluster sampling. Sampling is recommended for extremely large databases because it can significantly decrease model-training time. If the sample is sufficiently representative, relationships that are found in the sample can be expected to generalize to the complete data set. The Sampling node writes the sampled observations to an output data set and saves the seed values that are used to generate the random numbers for the samples so that you may replicate the samples.

The Data Partition node enables you to partition data sets into training, test, and validation data sets. The training data set is used for preliminary model fitting. The validation data set is used to monitor and tune the model weights during estimation and is also used for model assessment. The test data set is an additional holdout data set that you can use for model assessment. This node uses simple random sampling, stratified random sampling, or a user-defined partition to create training, validation, or test data sets. Specifying a user-defined partition indicates that you have determined which observations should be assigned to the training, validation, or test data sets, and this assignment is identified by a categorical variable that is in the raw data set.

Explore Nodes

The Distribution Explorer node is a visualization tool that enables you quickly and easily to explore large volumes of data in multidimensional histograms. You can view the distribution of up to three variables at a time with this node. When the variable is binary, nominal, or ordinal, you can select specific values to exclude from the chart. To exclude extreme values for interval variables, you can set a range cutoff. The node also generates simple descriptive statistics for the interval variables.

The Multiplot node is another visualization tool that enables you to explore larger volumes of data graphically. Unlike the Insight or Distribution Explorer nodes, the Multiplot node automatically creates bar charts and scatter plots for the input and target variables without making several menu or window item selections. The code that is created by this node can be used to create graphs in a batch environment, whereas the Insight and Distribution Explorer nodes must be run interactively.

The Insight node enables you to open a SAS/INSIGHT session. SAS/INSIGHT software is an interactive tool for data exploration and analysis. With it you explore samples of data through graphs and analyses that are linked across multiple windows. You can analyze univariate distributions, investigate multivariate distributions, and fit explanatory models by using generalized linear models.

The Association node enables you to identify association relationships within the data. For example, if a customer buys a loaf of bread, how likely is the customer to also buy a gallon of milk? The node also enables you to perform sequence discovery if a time stamp variable (a sequence variable) is present in the data set.

The Variable Selection node enables you to evaluate the importance of input variables in predicting or classifying the target variable. To select the important inputs, the node uses either an R-square or a Chi-square selection (tree based) criterion. The R-square criterion enables you to remove variables that have large percentages of missing values, remove class variables that are based on the number of unique values, and remove variables in hierarchies. Variables can be hierarchical because of levels of generalization (ZIPCODE generalizes to STATE, which generalizes to REGION) or because of formulation (variable A and variable B may have interaction A*B). The variables that are not related to the target are set to a status of rejected. Although rejected variables are passed to subsequent nodes in the process flow diagram, these variables are not used as model inputs by a more detailed modeling node, such as the Neural Network and Tree nodes. Certain variables of interest may be rejected by a variable selection technique, but you can force these variables into the model by reassigning these variables the input model role in any modeling node.

Modify Nodes

The Data set Attributes node enables you to modify data set attributes, such as data set names, descriptions, and roles. You can also use this node to modify the metadata sample that is associated with a data set and to specify target profiles for a target. An example of a useful Data Set Attributes application is to generate a data set in the SAS Code node and then modify its metadata sample with this node.

The Transform Variables node enables you to transform variables; for example, you can transform variables by taking the square root of a variable, by taking the natural logarithm, maximizing the correlation with the target, or normalizing a variable. Additionally, the node supports user-defined formulas for transformations and provides a visual interface for grouping interval-valued variables into buckets or quantiles. This node also automatically places interval variables into buckets by using a decision tree-based algorithm. Transforming variables to similar scale and variability may improve the fit of models and, subsequently, the classification and prediction precision of fitted models.

The Filter Outliers node enables you to identify and remove outliers from data sets. Checking for outliers is recommended, as outliers may greatly affect modeling results and, subsequently, the classification and prediction precision of fitted models.

The Replacement node enables you to impute (fill in) values for observations that have missing values. You can replace missing values for interval variables with the mean, median, midrange, mid-minimum spacing, or distribution-based replacement, or you can use a replacement M-estimator such as Tukey's biweight, Huber's, or Andrew's Wave. You can also estimate the replacement values for each interval input by using a tree-based imputation method. Missing values for class variables can be replaced with the most frequently occurring value, distribution-based replacement, tree-based imputation, or a constant.

The Clustering node enables you to segment your data; that is, it enables you to identify data observations that are similar in some way. Observations that are similar tend to be in the same cluster, and observations that are different tend to be in different clusters. The cluster identifier for each observation can be passed to other nodes for use as an input, ID, or target variable. It can also be passed as a group variable that enables you to automatically construct separate models for each group.

 The SOM/Kohonen node generates self-organizing maps, Kohonen networks, and vector quantization networks. Essentially the node performs unsupervised learning in which it attempts to learn the structure of the data. As with the Clustering node, after the network maps have been created, the characteristics can be examined graphically by using the results browser. The node provides the analysis results in the form of an interactive map that illustrates the characteristics of the clusters. Furthermore, it provides a report that indicates the importance of each variable.

Model Nodes

The Regression node enables you to fit both linear and logistic regression models to your data. You can use continuous, nominal, and binary target variables. You can use both continuous and discrete variables as inputs. The node supports the stepwise, forward, and backward-selection methods. A point-and-click interaction builder enables you to create higher-order modeling terms.

The Tree node enables you to perform multiway splitting of your database, based on nominal, ordinal, and continuous variables. This is the SAS System implementation of decision trees, which represents a hybrid of the best of CHAID, CART, and C4.5 algorithms. The node supports both automatic and interactive training. When you run the Tree node in automatic mode, it automatically ranks the input variables by the strength of their contribution to the tree. This ranking may be used to select variables for use in subsequent modeling. In addition, dummy variables can be generated for use in subsequent modeling. Using interactive training, you can override any automatic step by defining a splitting rule or by pruning a node or subtree.

The Neural Network node enables you to construct, train, and validate multilayer feed-forward neural networks. By default, the Neural Network node automatically constructs a multilayer feed-forward network that has one hidden layer consisting of three neurons. In general, each input is fully connected to the first hidden layer, each hidden layer is fully connected to the next hidden layer, and the last hidden layer is fully connected to the output. The Neural Network node supports many variations of this general form.

The User Defined Model node enables you to generate assessment statistics by using predicted values from a model that you built with the SAS Code node (for example, a logistic model that uses the SAS/STAT LOGISTIC procedure) or the Variable Selection node. You can also generate assessment statistics for models that are built by a third-party software product once you create a SAS data set that contains the predicted values from the model. The predicted values can also be saved to a SAS data set and then imported into the process flow with the Input Data Source node.

The Ensemble node creates a new model by averaging the posterior probabilities (for class targets) or the predicted values (for interval targets) from multiple models. The new model is then used to score new data.
One common ensemble approach is to resample the training data and fit a separate model for each sample. The Ensemble node then integrates the component models to form a potentially stronger solution.

Another common approach is to use multiple modeling methods, such as a neural network and a decision tree, to obtain separate models from the same training data set. The Ensemble node integrates the component models from the two complementary modeling methods to form the final model solution.

The Ensemble node can also be used to combine the scoring code from stratified models. The modeling nodes generate different scoring formulas when they operate on a stratification variable (for example, a group variable such as GENDER) that you define in a Group Processing node. The Ensemble node combines the scoring code into a single DATA step by logically dividing the data into IF-THEN-DO/END blocks.

It is important to note that the ensemble model that is created from either approach can be more accurate than the individual models only if the individual models disagree with one another.

Assess Nodes

The Assessment node provides a common framework for comparing models and predictions from any of the modeling nodes (Regression, Tree, Neural Network, and User Defined Model nodes). The comparison is based on the expected and actual profits or losses that would result from implementing the model. The node produces the following charts that help to describe the usefulness of the model: lift, profit, return on investment, receiver operating curves, diagnostic charts, and threshold-based charts.

The Score node enables you to generate and manage predicted values from a trained model. Scoring formulas are created for both assessment and prediction. Enterprise Miner generates and manages scoring formulas in the form of SAS DATA step code, which can usually be used in SAS even without the presence of Enterprise Miner.

The Reporter node assembles the results from a process flow analysis into an HTML report that can be viewed with your favorite Web browser. Each report contains header information, an image of the process flow diagram, and a separate report for each node in the flow including node settings and results. Reports are managed in the Reports tab of the Project Navigator.

Utility Nodes

The Group Processing node enables you to perform an analysis for each level of a class variable such as GENDER. You can also use this node to specify multiple targets or process the same data source repeatedly.   When multiple targets are selected, Enterprise Miner analyzes each target separately.

The Data Mining Database node enables you to create a data mining database (DMDB) for batch processing. For nonbatch processing, DMDBs are automatically created as they are needed.

The SAS Code node enables you to incorporate new or existing SAS code into process flow diagrams. The ability to write SAS code enables you to include additional SAS System procedures into your data mining analysis. You can also use a SAS DATA step to create customized scoring code, to conditionally process data, and to concatenate or to merge existing data sets. The node provides a macro facility to dynamically reference data sets (used for training, validation, testing, or for scoring) and variables, such as input, target, and predict variables. After you run the SAS Code node, the results and the data sets can then be exported for use by subsequent nodes in the diagram.

The Control Point node enables you to establish a control point to reduce the number of connections that are made in process flow diagrams. For example, suppose three Input Data Source nodes are to be connected to three modeling nodes. If no Control Point node is used, then nine connections are required to connect all of the Input Data Source nodes to all of the modeling nodes. However, if a Control Point node is used, only six connections are required.

The Subdiagram node enables you to group a portion of a process flow diagram into a subdiagram. For complex process flow diagrams, you may want to create subdiagrams to better design and control the process flow.

Some General Usage Rules for Nodes

These are some general rules that govern placing nodes in a process flow diagram (PFD):

- The Input Data Source cannot be preceded by any other node.

- The Sampling node must be preceded by a node that exports a data set.

- The Assessment node must be preceded by one or more modeling nodes.

- The Score node must be preceded by a node that produces score code. Any node that modifies the data or builds models generates score code.

- The SAS Code node can be defined in any stage of the process flow diagram. It does not require an input data set to be defined in the Input Data Source node.

1.3 Accessing Data in SAS Software

Using SAS Libraries

SAS uses libraries to organize files. These libraries point to folders where data and programs are stored. In Version 3 of Enterprise Miner, libraries must conform to the naming conventions that are used in Release 6.12. These conventions require the library name to have no more than eight alphanumeric characters, and the name cannot contain special characters such as asterisks (*) and ampersands (&). To create a new library or to view existing libraries, use the Globals menu and select **Access → Display libraries**.

You can see the files in a library by selecting the library name from the list of libraries in the upper-left portion of the dialog box. To create a new library, say CRSSAMP, select **New Library** and fill in the resulting dialog box with the desired library name and associated path. The following library identifies the folder whose path is `C:\workshop\bsd\dmem`.

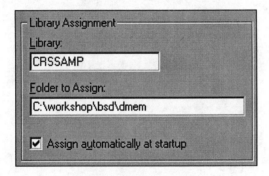

Observe that the box for **Assign automatically at startup** is checked. This library will be reassigned every time that the SAS session starts. If you do not check this box, the library name is not automatically assigned when the SAS or Enterprise Miner session starts. As a result, the contents of the library will be unavailable for use by the SAS System or Enterprise Miner in future sessions unless you reassign the library name manually. Select **Assign** to finish assigning the library name.

There are several libraries that are automatically assigned when you open Enterprise Miner. One of these libraries (SAMPSIO) contains sample data sets that are used in Enterprise Miner reference material to illustrate important concepts. For the purposes of this document, assume that the data sets are in SAMPSIO. Any data set in the library can then be referenced by the two-part name that is constructed by using the SAS library name and the SAS data set name. For example, the HMEQ data set in the SAMPSIO library is identified by the two-part name SAMPSIO.HMEQ.

Chapter 2: Predictive Modeling

2.1 Problem Formulation

Overview

A financial services company offers a home equity line of credit to its clients. The company has extended several thousand lines of credit in the past, and many of these accepted applicants (approximately 20%) have defaulted. By using geographic, demographic, and financial variables, the company wants to build a model to predict whether an applicant will default. This is an example of a predictive modeling problem.

The Data

After analyzing the data, the company selected a subset of 12 predictor (or input) variables to model whether each applicant defaulted. The response (or outcome) variable indicates whether an applicant defaulted on the home equity line of credit (BAD). The variables, along with their model role, measurement level, and description, are shown in the table below. Note: This table was not created with Enterprise Miner software.

Name	Model Role	Measurement Level	Description
BAD	Target	Binary	1=client defaulted on loan, 0=loan repaid
CLAGE	Input	Interval	Age of oldest trade line in months
CLNO	Input	Interval	Number of trade lines
DEBTINC	Input	Interval	Debt-to-income ratio
DELINQ	Input	Interval	Number of trade lines
DEROG	Input	Interval	Number of major derogatory reports
JOB	Input	Nominal	Six occupational categories
LOAN	Input	Binary	Amount of the loan request
MORTDUE	Input	Interval	Amount due on existing mortgage
NINQ	Input	Interval	Number of recent credit inquiries
REASON	Input	Binary	DebtCon=debt consolidation, HomeImp=home improvement
VALUE	Input	Interval	Value of current property
YOJ	Input	Interval	Years at present job

The HMEQ data set in the SAMPSIO library contains 5,960 observations for building and comparing competing models. This data set will be split into training, validation, and test data sets for analysis.

2.2 Building a Sample Flow

Building the Flow

Begin building the first flow to analyze this data. Use the toolbar to access the commonly used nodes. You can add additional nodes to the toolbar by dragging the nodes from the Tools tab to the toolbar. All of the nodes will remain available in the Tools tab.

Add an Input Data Source node by dragging the node from the toolbar or from the Tools tab. Since this is a predictive modeling flow, add a Data Partition node to the right of the Input Data Source node. In addition to dragging a node onto the workspace, there are two other ways to add a node to the flow. You can right-click in the workspace in which you want the node to appear and select **Add node** from the pop-up menu that appears, or you can double-click where you want the node to appear. In either case, a list of nodes appears, and you need only to select the desired node. After you select **Data Partition**, your diagram should look as follows.

Input Data
Source

Data
Partition

Observe that the Data Partition node is selected (as indicated by the dotted line around it) but the Input Data Source node is not. If you click in any open space on the workspace, all nodes become deselected.

Using the Cursor

The shape of the cursor changes depending on where it is positioned. The behavior of the mouse commands depends on the shape as well as the selection state of the node over which the cursor is positioned. Right-click in an open area to see the menu. The last three menu items (Connect items, Move items, Move and Connect) enable you to modify the ways in which the cursor may be used. The Move and Connect item is selected by default as indicated by the asterisk that appears next to it. It is recommended that you do not change this setting, as it is more convenient and efficient to use the mouse to perform both tasks without the need to toggle between cursor settings. If your cursor is not performing a desired task, check this menu to make sure that the Move and Connect item is selected. This selection enables you to move the nodes around the workspace as well as to connect them.

Observe that when you put your cursor in the middle of a node, the cursor appears as a hand. You can move the nodes around the workspace as follows:
1. Position the cursor in the middle of the node (until the hand appears).
2. Press the left mouse button and drag the node to the desired location.
3. Release the left mouse button.

Note that after you drag a node, the node remains selected. To deselect all of the nodes, click in an open area of the workspace. Also note that when you put the cursor on the outside edge of the node, the cursor appears as a cross-hair. You can connect the node where the cursor is positioned (beginning node) to any other node (ending node) as follows:

1. Ensure that the beginning node is deselected. It is much easier to drag a line when the node is deselected. If the beginning node is selected, click in an open area of the workspace to deselect it.
2. Position the cursor on the edge of the icon that represents the beginning node (until the cross-hair appears).
3. Press the left mouse button and immediately begin to drag in the direction of the ending node. Note: If you do not begin dragging immediately after pressing the left mouse button, you will only select the node. Dragging a selected node will generally result in moving the node (that is, no line will form).
4. Release the mouse button after you reach the edge of the icon that represents the ending node.
5. Click away from the arrow. Initially, the connection will appear as follows. After you click away from the line in an open area of the workspace, the finished arrow forms.

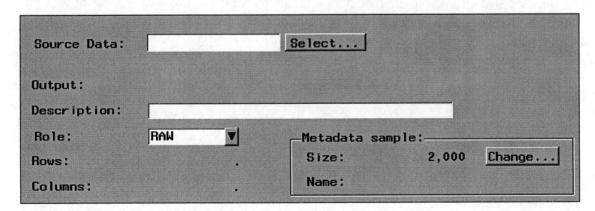

Identifying the Input Data

The first example uses the HMEQ data set in the SAMPSIO library. To specify the input data, double-click on the Input Data Source node or right-click on this node and select **Open**. The Data tab is active. Your window should look like the one below.

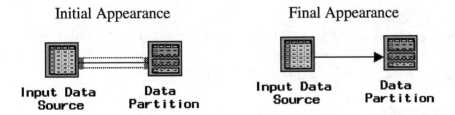

Click on **Select** in order to select the data set. Alternatively, you can enter the name of the data set.

The SASUSER library is selected by default. To view data sets in the SAMPSIO library, click on the ▼ and select SAMPSIO from the list of defined libraries.

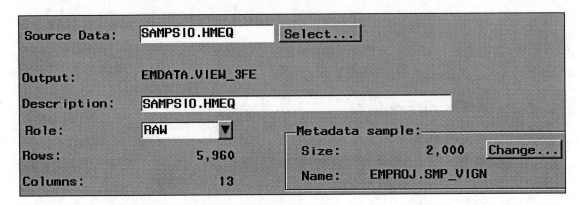

Select the HMEQ data set from the list of data sets in the SAMPSIO library, and then select **OK**. The resulting dialog appears below.

Observe that this data set has 5,960 observations (rows) and 13 variables (columns). Observe that the field next to **Source Data:** contains SAMPSIO.HMEQ. You could have typed in this name instead of selecting it through the dialog box. Note that the lower-right corner indicates a metadata sample of size 2,000. The next section explains the metadata sample.

Understanding the Metadata Sample

All analysis packages must determine how to use variables in the analysis. Enterprise Miner uses metadata in order to make a preliminary assessment of how to use each variable. By default, it takes a random sample of 2,000 observations from the data set of interest, and uses this information to assign a model role and a measurement level to each variable. It also computes simple descriptive statistics that are displayed under additional tabs. If you want to take a larger sample, you may select **Change** in the metadata sample area of the dialog box (lower right corner), but this change is unneccessary in most cases and it is not shown here.

Evaluate (and update, if necessary) the assignments that were made using the metadata sample. Click on the **Variables** tab to see all of the variables and their respective assignments. You can see all of the variables if you maximize the window. The following table shows a portion of the information for each of the 13 variables in this example.

Name	Model Role	Measurement	Type	Format
BAD	input	binary	num	BEST12.
LOAN	input	interval	num	BEST12.
MORTDUE	input	interval	num	BEST12.
VALUE	input	interval	num	BEST12.
REASON	input	binary	char	$7.
JOB	input	nominal	char	$7.
YOJ	input	interval	num	BEST12.
DEROG	input	ordinal	num	BEST12.
DELINQ	input	ordinal	num	BEST12.
CLAGE	input	interval	num	BEST12.
NINQ	input	interval	num	BEST12.
CLNO	input	interval	num	BEST12.
DEBTINC	input	interval	num	BEST12.

Observe that the Name and Type columns are not available (they appear dimmed). These columns represent information from the SAS data set that cannot be changed in this node. The Name must conform to the naming conventions that are described earlier for libraries. The Type is either character (char) or numeric (num) and affects how a variable can be used. Enterprise Miner uses the value for Type and the number of levels in the metadata sample to initially assign a model role and measurement level to each variable.

The first variable listed is BAD. Although BAD is a numeric variable in the data set, Enterprise Miner identifies it as a *binary* variable since it has only two distinct non-missing levels in the metadata sample. The model role for all *binary* variables is set to *input* by default.

The next three variables (LOAN, MORTDUE, and VALUE) are assigned an *interval* measurement level since they are numeric variables in the SAS data set and have more than ten distinct levels in the metadata sample. The model role for all *interval* variables is set to *input* by default.

The variables REASON and JOB are both character variables in the data set, yet they have different measurement levels. REASON is assigned a *binary* measurement level because it has only two distinct nonmissing levels in the metadata sample. JOB, however, is assigned a *nominal* measurement level since it is a character variable with more than two levels. The model role for all *binary* and *nominal* variables is set to *input* by default.

For the purpose of this analysis, treat the remaining variables (YOJ through DEBTINC) as interval variables. Notice that in the table, DEROG and DELINQ have been assigned an *ordinal* measurement level. This assignment occurs because each is a numeric variable with more than two, but not more than ten distinct nonmissing levels in the metadata sample. This often occurs in variables that contain counts (such as number of children). Since this assignment depends on the number of levels for each variable in the metadata sample, the measurement level of DEROG or DELINQ for the analysis may be set to *interval*. The model role for all *ordinal* variables is set to *input* by default.

Identifying Target Variables

Because BAD is the response variable for this analysis, change the model role for BAD to *target*. To modify the model role information for BAD, proceed as follows:
1. Position the tip of your cursor over the row for BAD in the model role column and right-click.
2. Select **Set Model Role → target** from the pop-up menu.

Inspecting Distributions

You can inspect the distribution of values in the metadata sample for each of the variables. To view the distribution of BAD, for example, proceed as follows:
1. Position the tip of your cursor over the variable BAD in the Name column.
2. Right-click and observe that you can Sort by name, Find name, or View distribution of BAD.
3. Select **View distribution** to see the distribution of values for BAD in the metadata sample.

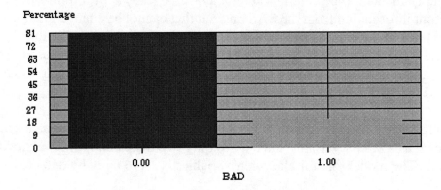

To obtain additional information, select the the View Info tool ( ) from the toolbar at the top of the window and click one of the histogram bars. Enterprise Miner displays the level and the proportion of observations that are represented by the bar. These plots provide an initial overview of the data. For this example, approximately 20% of the observations were loans for which the client defaulted (BAD=1).

Recall that the plots and statistics in the Input Data Source node are based on the metadata sample, so the exact values in your window may differ slightly from those displayed here. These differences will not appear later in the modeling results since the modeling nodes use the entire training dataset and not just a sample.

Select **Close** to return to the main dialog box when you are finished inspecting the plot.

Modifying Variable Information

Ensure that the remaining variables have the correct model role and measurement level information as shown in the first table in the problem formulation section (Section 2.1). If necessary, change the measurement level for DEROG and DELINQ to interval. To modify the measurement level information for DEROG, proceed as follows:

1. Position the tip of your cursor over the row for DEROG in the measurement level column and right-click.
2. Select **Set Measurement Level → interval** from the pop-up menu.
3. Repeat steps 1 and 2 for DELINQ.

Alternatively, you could have updated the model role information for both variables simultaneously by highlighting the rows for both DEROG and DELINQ before following steps 1 and 2 above.

Investigating Descriptive Statistics

The metadata is used to compute descriptive statistics. To begin, select the **Interval Variables** tab.

Name	Min	Max	Mean	Std Dev.	Missing %
LOAN	1500	89800	18792	10745	0%
MORTDUE	4000	399412	74783	44481	9%
VALUE	8800	854114	103389	60122	2%
YOJ	0	41	8.7928	7.451	9%
DEROG	0	9	0.2519	0.8872	12%
DELINQ	0	13	0.4181	1.0832	10%
CLAGE	0	1154.6	181.07	89.05	5%
NINQ	0	12	1.1625	1.6759	9%
CLNO	0	71	21.456	10.267	4%
DEBTINC	1.9092	203.31	33.969	9.5665	20%

Investigate the minimum value, maximum value, mean, standard deviation, percentage of missing observations, skewness, and kurtosis for interval variables. In this example, an inspection of the minimum and maximum values indicates no unusual values. Observe that DEBTINC has a high percentage of missing values (20%). Select the **Class Variables** tab.

Name	Values	Missing %	Order
BAD	2	0%	Ascending
REASON	2	4%	Ascending
JOB	6	5%	Ascending

Investigate the number of levels, percentage of missing values, and the sort order of each variable. The sort order for BAD is descending, while the sort order for all the others is ascending. For a binary target such as BAD, the first sorted level is the target event. Since BAD has two levels (0 and 1) and BAD is sorted in descending order, BAD=1 is the target event. You may need to change the sort order to get the target event that you want. Close the Input Data Source node, and save changes when you are prompted.

Inspecting Default Settings in the Data Partition Node

Open the Data Partition node. The Partition tab is active by default. The partition method options are found in the upper-left corner of the Partition tab.

By default, Enterprise Miner takes a simple random sample of the input data and divides it into training, validation, and test data sets. You can generate stratified samples or implement previously implemented user-defined samples as follows:
- Stratified sampling - select the Stratified radio button and then use the options in the Stratified tab to set up your strata.
- User Defined sampling - select the User Defined button and then use the options in the User Defined tab to identify the variable in the data set that identifies the partitions.

The lower-left corner of the tab enables you to specify a random seed for initializing the sampling process. Randomization within computer programs is often started by some type of seed. If you use the same data set with the same seed in different flows, you get the same partition. Observe that re-sorting the data results in a different ordering of data. Therefore, a different partition yields potentially different results.

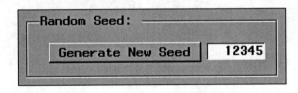

The right side of the tab enables you to specify the percentage of the data to allocate to training, validation, and test data.

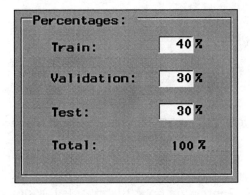

Use the default settings for this example. Close the Data Partition node. If you did not make changes, you will not be prompted to save changes. If you are prompted to save changes when you close this node, select **No** to retain the default settings of the Data Partition node.

Understanding Data Replacement

Add a Replacement node to the diagram. This allows you to replace missing values for each variable. This replacement is necessary to use all of the observations in the training data set when you build a regression or neural network model. Decision trees handle missing values directly, while regression and neural network models ignore all incomplete observations (observations with a missing value for one or more input variable). It is more appropriate to compare models that are built on the same set of observations, so you should perform this replacement before fitting any regression or neural network model when you plan to compare the results to those obtained from a decision tree model.

By default, Enterprise Miner uses a sample from the training data set to select the values for replacement. Observations with a missing value for an

- *interval* variable have the missing value replaced with the mean of the sample for the corresponding variable.
- *binary*, *nominal*, or *ordinal* variable have the missing value replaced with the most commonly occurring nonmissing level of the corresponding variable in the sample.

Your new diagram should appear as follows:

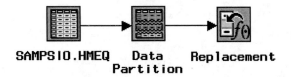

Fitting a Regression Model

Add a Regression node to the workspace and connect it from the Replacement node. The diagram should now appear as follows:

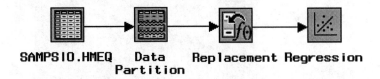

SAMPSIO.HMEQ   Data   Replacement Regression
Partition

Modeling nodes, such as the Regression node, require you to specify a target variable in the Input Data Source. The Regression node fits models for interval, ordinal, and binary targets. Since you selected a binary variable (BAD) as the target in the Input Data Source node, the Regression node will fit (by default) a binary logistic regression model with main effects for each input variable. The node also codes your grouping variables with either GLM (or *dummy*) coding or Deviation (or *effect*) coding. By default, the node uses Deviation coding for categorical input variables..

Evaluating the Model

Add an Assessment node to the diagram. Your flow should now look as follows:

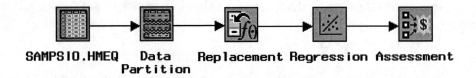

SAMPSIO.HMEQ   Data   Replacement Regression Assessment
Partition

Right-click on the Assessment node and select **Run**. Observe that each node becomes green as it runs. Since you ran the flow from the Assessment node, you will be prompted to see the Assessment results when Enterprise Miner completes its processing. View the results when you are prompted and select **Tools → Lift Chart**.

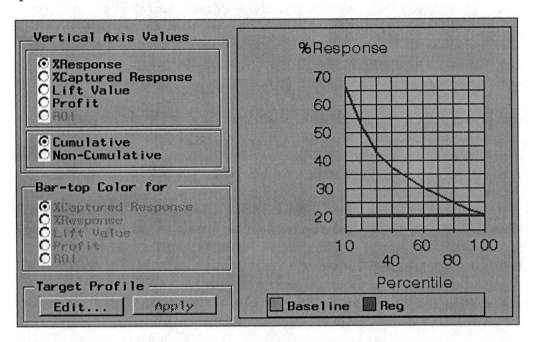

A Cumulative %Response chart appears first. By default, this chart arranges individuals into deciles based on their predicted probability of response, and then plots the actual percentage of respondents. To see actual values, select the **View Info** tool (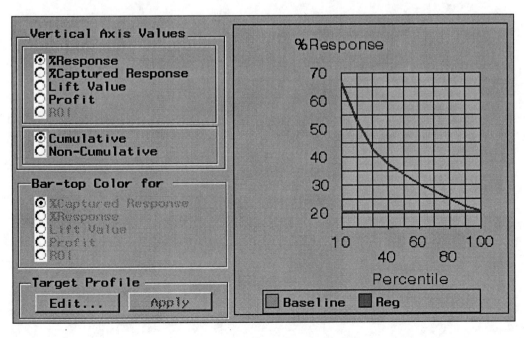) from the toolbar and then left-click on the red line. Clicking on the red line near the upper-left corner of the plot indicates a %Response of 65.88.

To interpret the Cumulative %Response chart, consider how the chart is constructed.

1. For this example, the response of interest is loan defaults; thus, a respondent is defined as a individual who defaults on a loan (BAD=1). For each individual, the fitted model (in this case, a regression model) predicts the probability that the individual will default. The observations are sorted by the predicted probability of response from the highest probability of response to the lowest probability of response.
2. The observations are then grouped into ordered bins, each containing approximately 10% of the data.
3. Using the target variable BAD, count the percentage of actual respondents in each bin.

If the model is useful, the proportion of individuals with the event level that you are modeling (in this example, those who defaulted on a loan) will be relatively high in bins in which the predicted probability of response is high. The cumulative response curve that is shown above shows the percentage of respondents in the top 10%, top 20%, top 30%, and so on.

In the top 10%, almost two-thirds of the individuals had defaulted on a loan. In the top 20%, just over half had defaulted on the loan. The horizontal blue line represents the baseline rate (approximately 20%) for comparison purposes, which is an estimate of the percentage of defaulters that you would expect if you were to take a random sample. The default plot represents cumulative percentages, but you can also see the proportion of those who defaulted in each bin by selecting the radio button next to Non-Cumulative on the left side of the graph.

The discussion of the remaining charts refers to those who defaulted on a loan as *defaulters* or *respondents*. In the previous plot, the percentage of defaulters was 65.88% in the first decile. In other words, 65.88% of those in the first decile had the target event of interest (BAD=1).

Select the radio button next to Non-Cumulative and inspect the resulting plot.

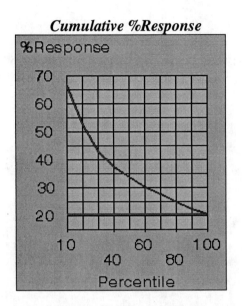

Cumulative %Response

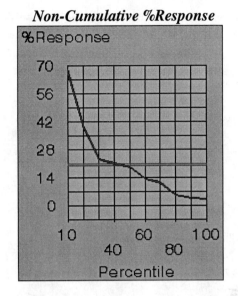

Non-Cumulative %Response

Both plots are displayed to allow further comparison. The noncumulative plot shows the percentage of defaulters in each decile. The cumulative plot can be obtained from averaging the appropriate percentages in the noncumulative plot. For example, the 20th percentile in the Cumulative %Response plot can be calculated from averaging the percent response in the top two deciles of the Non-Cumulative %Response plot. Next select the **Cumulative** button and then select **Lift Value**.

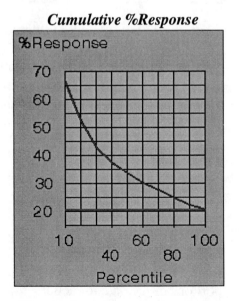

Cumulative %Response

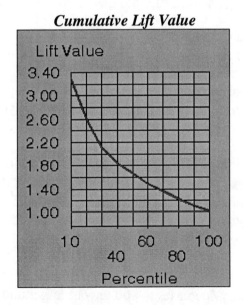

Cumulative Lift Value

Lift charts plot the same information on a different scale. The overall response rate is 20%. Calculate *lift* by dividing the response rate in a given group by the overall response rate. The percentage of respondents in the first decile was 65.88%. Dividing 65.88% by 20% (overall response rate) gives a lift slightly higher than three, which indicates that the response rate in the first decile is over three times as high as the response rate in the population.

Instead of asking the question, "What percentage of those in a bin were defaulters?", you could ask the question, "What percentage of the total number of defaulters are in a bin?" The latter question can be evaluated by using the Captured Response curve. To inspect this curve, select the radio button next to %Captured Response. Use the View Info tool to evaluate how the model performs.

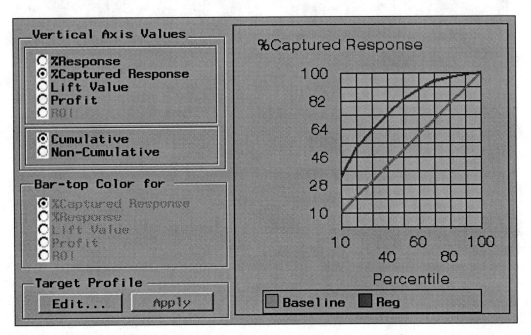

You can calculate lift from this type of chart as well. If you were to take a random sample of 10% of the observations, you would expect to capture 10% of the defaulters. Likewise, if you take a random sample of 20% of the data, you would expect to capture 20% of the defaulters. You can calculate lift, therefore, by dividing the proportion of the defaulters that you have captured by the percentage of those whom you have chosen for action (rejection of the loan application).

Observe that if the percentage of applications chosen for rejection were approximately
- 20%, you would have identified about 50% of those who would have defaulted, which corresponds to a lift of about 50/20=2.5.
- 30%, you would have identified over 60% of those who would have defaulted, which corresponds to a lift of over 60/30=2.

Observe that lift depends on the proportion of those who have been chosen for action. Lift generally decreases as you choose larger and larger proportions of the data for action. When comparing two models on the same proportion of the data, the model with the higher lift is often preferred (barring issues that involve model complexity and interpretability).

Note: A model that performs best in the one decile may perform poorly at other deciles; therefore, when you compare competing models, your choice of the final model may depend on the proportion of individuals that you have chosen for action.

2.3 Data Preparation and Investigation

Preliminary Investigation

Recall that the Insight node provides you with point-and-click access to many powerful statistical graphics that are useful for preliminary investigation. You can add an Insight node to the workspace and connect it to the Data Partition node as illustrated below.

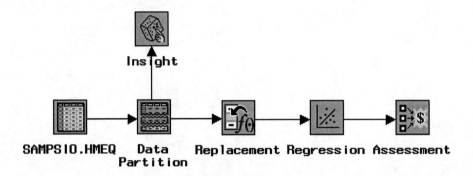

SAMPSIO.HMEQ   Data   Replacement Regression Assessment
               Partition

Run the flow from the Insight node by right-clicking on Insight and selecting **Run**. Select **Yes** when you are prompted to see the results. A portion of the output is shown below.

▶ 13	Int	Int	Int	Int	Nom	Nom	Int
2000	BAD	LOAN	MORTDUE	VALUE	REASON	JOB	YOJ
1	1	1100	25860.00	39025.00	HomeImp	Other	10.50
2	1	1500	13500.00	16700.00	HomeImp	Other	4.00
3	1	1500	.	.			.
4	1	1800	28502.00	43034.00	HomeImp	Other	11.00
5	1	2000	32700.00	46740.00	HomeImp	Other	3.00
6	1	2000	.	62250.00	HomeImp	Sales	16.00
7	1	2000	20627.00	29800.00	HomeImp	Office	11.00
8	1	2000	45000.00	55000.00	HomeImp	Other	3.00
9	0	2000	64536.00	87400.00		Mgr	2.50
10	1	2100	71000.00	83850.00	HomeImp	Other	8.00

Observe that the upper-left corner contains the numbers 2000 and 13, which indicates there are 2,000 rows (observations) and 13 columns (variables). This represents a sample from either the training data set or the validation data set, but how would you know which one? Close Insight to return to the workspace.

Open the Insight node by right-clicking on the node in the workspace and selecting **Open**. The Data tab is initially active. An example is displayed below.

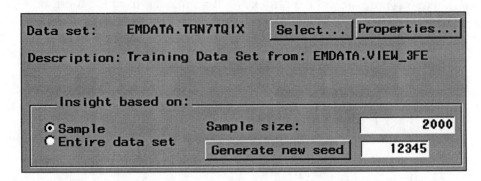

Observe that the selected data set is the training data set. The name of the data set, EMDATA.TRN7TQIX, is composed of key letters (in this case, TRN) and some random alphanumeric characters (in this case, 7TQIX) and is stored in the EMDATA library. The bottom of the tab indicates that Insight is generating a random sample of 2,000 observations from the training data based on the random seed 12345.

Since the naming process involves random assignment, the name of your data set will almost certainly be different; however, Enterprise Miner assigns the SAS library name EMDATA to the folder that contains these files. If you create a new project, these files will be placed in a different folder, but the SAS library name will still be EMDATA. This does not cause a conflict since you can have only one project open at one time. When opening a different project, Enterprise Miner reassigns the EMDATA library name to the appropriate folder for that project.

To change the data set that Insight is using, click on **Select** next to the data set name. Inspect the resulting Imports Map dialog.

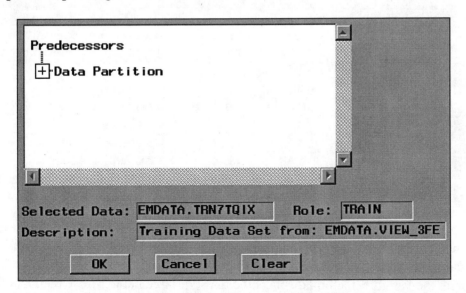

Data Partition is listed under Predecessors since the Data Partition node is connected to Insight. The Data Partition node is the only predecessor.

Click on the ⊞ next to Data Partition and then click on the ⊞ next to SAS_DATA_SETS. Three data sets are shown that represent the training (TRN*abcde*), validation (VAL*abcde*), and test data sets (TST*abcde*). Note: These are not the only key letters that are used for training, validation, and test data sets. If you click on a SAS data set, the type of partition is displayed in the description field below the tree diagram.

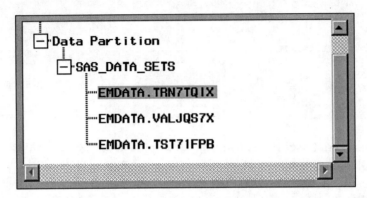

Select **OK** from the bottom of the Imports Map dialog box to return to the Data tab.

Data set:	EMDATA.TRN7TQIX	Select...	Properties...

Description: Training Data Set from: EMDATA.VIEW_3FE

Click on the **Properties** button as shown above. The Data Set Details dialog box appears, and the Information tab is active. This tab provides information about when the data set was constructed as well as the number of rows and columns it contains. Select the **Table View** tab.

☑ Variable labels

	BAD	LOAN	MORTDUE	VALUE	REASON	JOB	YOJ
1	1	1100	25860	39025	Homelmp	Other	10.5
2	1	1500	13500	16700	Homelmp	Other	4
3	1	1500	.	.			.
4	1	1800	28502	43034	Homelmp	Other	11
5	1	2000	32700	46740	Homelmp	Other	3
6	1	2000	.	62250	Homelmp	Sales	16
7	1	2000	20627	29800	Homelmp	Office	11
8	1	2000	45000	55000	Homelmp	Other	3

This tab enables you to view the data for the currently selected data set in tabular form. The check box enables you to see the column headings that use the variable labels. Unchecking the box would cause the table to use the SAS variable names for column headings. If no label is associated with the variable, the box displays the SAS variable name. Close the Data Set Details window when you are finished to return to the main Insight dialog box.

Select the radio button next to **Entire data set** to run Insight on the entire data set.

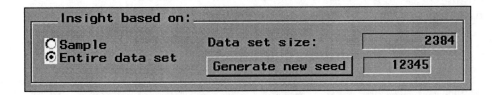

Note: Do not load extremely large data tables into Insight. If the data table is very large, using Insight on a moderate sample instead is usually sufficient to explore the data.

You can run Insight with the new settings by proceeding as follows:
1. Close the Insight dialog window.
2. Select **Yes** when you are prompted to save changes.
3. Run the diagram from the Insight node.
4. Select **Yes** when you are prompted to see the results.

Note: You can also run Insight without closing the Insight dialog box by selecting the run icon (
) from the toolbar and selecting **Yes** when you are prompted to see the results.

Before proceeding, check to ensure that the Insight window is in fact the active window. From the menus at the top of Enterprise Miner, select **Window→EMDATA.<data-set-name>** (TRN7TQIX, in this example). Investigate the distribution of each of the variables as follows:
1. From the menus at the top of the Insight window, select **Analyze→Distribution (Y)**
2. Highlight all of the variables in the variable list.
3. Select **Y**.
4. Select **OK**.

Charts for continuous variables include histograms, box and whisker plots, and assorted descriptive statistics. A portion of the output for the variable LOAN is shown below.

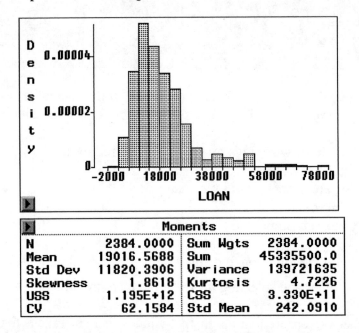

Scroll through the output until you reach the graph for REASON. The unlabeled level represents observations that have a missing value for REASON.

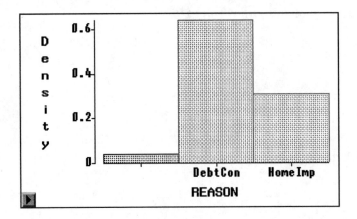

Now scroll down and inspect the distribution of YOJ (which is very skewed) and DEROG (which has a large proportion of observations at DEROG=0). Observe that DEROG has relatively few observations in which DEROG > 0.

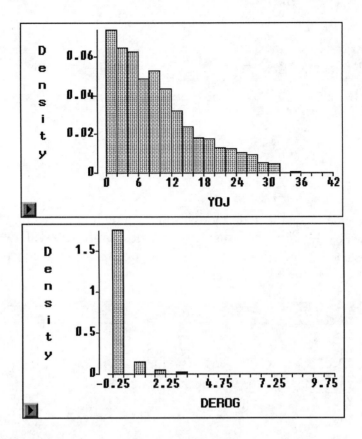

When you are finished, return to the main process flow diagram as follows:
1. Close the distribution window when you are finished.
2. Close the Insight data table.
3. If you ran Insight without closing the node, close the Insight node (saving changes if you are prompted).

Performing Variable Transformations

After you have viewed the results in Insight, it is clear that some input variables have highly skewed distributions. In highly skewed distributions, a small percentage of the points may have a great deal of influence. On occasion, performing a transformation on an input variable may yield a better fitting model. This section demonstrates how to perform some common transformations.

Add a Transform Variables node to the flow as shown below.

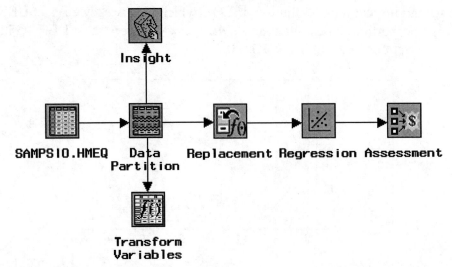

After connecting the node, open the node by right-clicking on it and selecting **Open**. The Variables tab is shown by default, which displays statistics for the interval level variables including the mean, standard deviation, skewness, and kurtosis (calculated from the metadata sample).

Name	Keep	Formula	Mean	Std Dev	Skew	Kurtosis
LOAN	Yes		19114.25	11914.61	1.82	4.43
MORTDUE	Yes		74708.97	45846.55	1.85	6.60
VALUE	Yes		103841.4	60534.26	3.43	28.23
YOJ	Yes		9.071198	7.628394	0.99	0.38
DEROG	Yes		0.22919	0.813416	5.71	43.36
DELINQ	Yes		0.464444	1.172628	4.15	24.34
CLAGE	Yes		183.5176	86.60054	0.99	2.36
NINQ	Yes		1.189665	1.697336	2.44	8.01
CLNO	Yes		21.62461	10.24814	0.74	1.02
DEBTINC	Yes		33.58185	8.09904	1.12	22.33

The Transform Variables node enables you to rapidly transform interval valued variables by using standard transformations. You can also create new variables whose values are calculated from existing variables in the data set. Observe that the only available column in this dialog box is the Keep column. You can edit formulas for calculated columns by right-clicking on the appropriate row or by using the Actions pull-down menu.

You can view the distribution of each variable just as you did in the Input Data Source node. Position the tip of your cursor on the row for YOJ and right-click. Select **View Distribution** from the menu. Begin by viewing the distribution of YOJ.

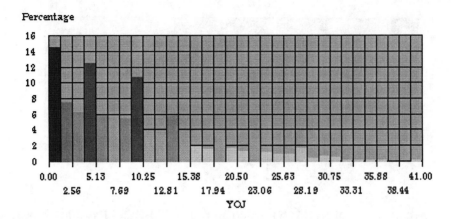

Consider a log transformation of YOJ. This transformation is one of several one-step transformations that are available in the Transform Variables node. After closing the graph of YOJ, create a new variable by taking the log of YOJ. To do so, proceed as follows:

1. Position your cursor over the row for YOJ.
2. Right-click and select **Transform → Log**.
3. Observe that a new variable has been added to the dialog window.

Name	Keep	Formula	Mean	Std Dev	Skew
LOAN	Yes		19114.25	11914.61	1.82
MORTDUE	Yes		74708.97	45846.55	1.85
VALUE	Yes		103841.4	60534.26	3.43
YOJ	No		9.071198	7.628394	0.99
YOJ_V3N0	Yes	log((YOJ + 1))	1.966028	0.910616	-0.54

The name of the new variable is composed of some key letters from the original variable (YOJ) and some random alphanumeric characters (V3N0). Observe that the original variable has Keep=No while the newly created variable has Keep=Yes. This indicates that the original variable (YOJ) will no longer be available in any node connected after this Transform Variables node. Do not modify the values of Keep now.

The formula shows that Enterprise Miner has performed the log transformation after adding one to the value of YOJ. To understand why this has occurred, recall that YOJ has a minimum value of zero. The logarithm of zero is undefined, and the logarithm of something close to zero is extremely negative. Enterprise Miner takes this information into account and uses the transformation log(YOJ+1) to create a new variable that has values that are greater than or equal to zero (since the log(1)=0).

Inspect the distribution of the new variable, which is labeled log(YOJ).

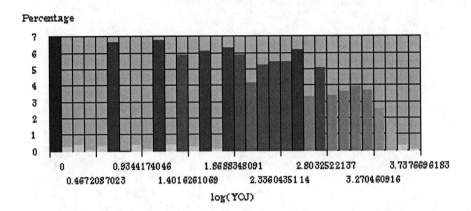

Now view the distribution of DEROG. The distribution of DEROG has a large proportion of observations at DEROG=0 and relatively few in which DEROG > 0.

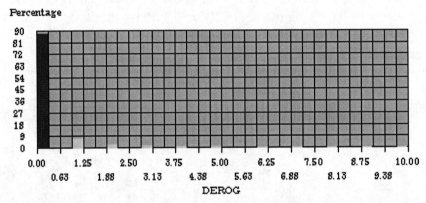

After viewing the distribution of DEROG, close the plot and view the distribution of DELINQ.

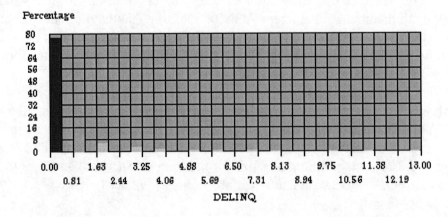

The same pattern that holds for DEROG also holds for DELINQ. In situations in which there is a large mass of points at one value and relatively few points spread out over the rest of the space, it is sometimes useful to group the levels of an interval variable.

Instead of fitting a slope to the whole range of values for DEROG or DELINQ, the problem reduces to estimating the mean in each group. Since most of the applicants in the data set had no delinquent credit lines, there is a high concentration of points at DELINQ=0. Close the plot when you are finished inspecting it.

Create a new variable INDEROG which indicates whether or not DEROG is greater than 0. Repeat the process for DELINQ but name the new variable INDELINQ.

To create the variable INDEROG, proceed as follows:

1. Select **Actions → Create Variable** (alternately, you can click on the 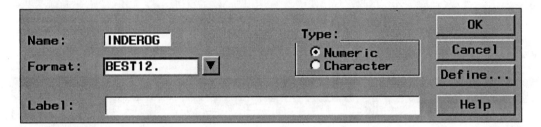 on the toolbar).
2. Type INDEROG in the name field.

3. Select **Define**.
4. Type in the formula DEROG > 0 as shown below.

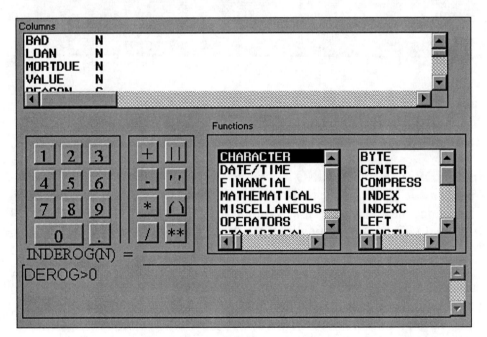

This definition is an example of Boolean logic and illustrates a way to dichotimize an interval variable. The statement is either true or false for each observation. When the statement is true, the expression evaluates as 1; otherwise, the expression evaluates as 0. In other words, when DEROG>0, INDEROG=1. Likewise, when DEROG≤0, INDEROG=0. If the value of DEROG is missing, the expression evaluates as 0, since missing values are treated as being smaller than any nonmissing value in a numerical comparison. Since a missing value of DEROG is reasonably imputed as DEROG=0, this does not pose a problem fot his example.

5. Select **OK**. Observe that the formula now appears in the Formula window.

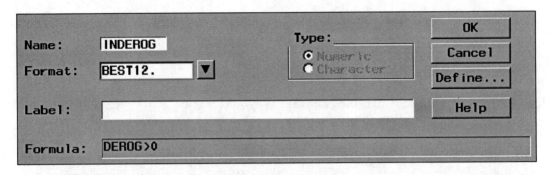

6. Select **OK**. The new variable, INDEROG, now appears in the list.

Name	Keep	Formula	Mean	Std Dev	Skew
INDEROG	Yes	DEROG>0	0.107	0.309191	2.54

7. Repeat the steps for INDELINQ.

Name	Keep	Formula	Mean	Std Dev	Skew
INDELINQ	Yes	DELINQ>0	0.2035	0.402702	1.47
INDEROG	Yes	DEROG>0	0.107	0.309191	2.54

Note that missing values of DELINQ result in INDELINQ=0 (see step 4 above). Since it is reasonable to impute DELINQ=0 when the value of DELINQ is missing, this does not pose a problem for this variable either.

Observe that even though DEROG and DELINQ were used to construct the new variables, the original variables are still available for analysis (Keep=Yes). You can modify this if you want, but that is not done here since the created variables contain only a portion of the information that is contained in DEROG and DELINQ; specifically, they identify whether DEROG or DELINQ is greater than zero.

Examine the distribution of NINQ. NINQ is a counting variable, but the majority of the observations have values of 0, 1, or 2. It may be useful to create a grouped version of NINQ by pooling all of the values larger than 2 (of which there are very few) into a new level "2+". This would create a new three-level grouping variable from NINQ. While creating a grouping variable with three levels causes loss of information about the exact number of recent credit inquiries, it does enable you to handle nonlinearity in the relationship between NINQ and the response of interest.

First, create a new grouping variable that creates bins for the values of NINQ. You can create a grouping variable by using several different methods including the following:
1. Bucket - creates cutoffs at approximately equally spaced intervals.
2. Quantile - creates bins with approximately equal frequencies.
3. Optimal Binning for Relationship to Target - creates cutoffs that yield optimal relationship to target (for binary targets).

The Optimal Binning for Relationship to Target transformation uses the DMSPLIT procedure to optimally split a variable into n groups with regard to a binary target. To create the n optimal groups, the procedure performs a recursive process of splitting the variable into groups that maximize the association with the target variable. The node uses the metadata to determine the optimum groups to speed processing. This binning transformation is useful when there is a nonlinear relationship between the input variable and a binary target. Enterprise Miner assigns an ordinal measurement level to the newly created variable. For more information, see the Online Reference Help for the Transform Variables node in Enterprise Miner.

Enterprise Miner provides help on a large number of topics in Help files that are organized for easy access. For example, to obtain software-based Help on binning transformations, proceed as follows:
1. Select **Help → Enterprise Miner Reference**. The Contents tab should be active. If it is not, select **Contents**.
2. Double-click on the book icon titled **Enterprise Miner Version X.x Reference Help,** where X.x refers to your currently installed version of Enterprise Miner. Note: Optionally, select the book icon and then select **Open**.
3. Scroll down the window to the Transform Variables node.
4. Double-click on the **Transform Variables Node**.
    Note: Optionally, select **Transform Variables Node** and then select **Display**.
5. Select **Creating Transformed variables**.
6. Select **Binning Transformations**.
7. Close the Help window when you are finished.

Suppose you wanted to bin the values of NINQ into 0, 1, and 2+ (2 or more). To create the new binning variable, proceed as follows:
1. Position your cursor over the row for NINQ.
2. Right-click and select **Transform → Bucket**.
    Note: Optionally, select the **Transform → Quantile**.
3. The default number of buckets is 4. Change this value to 3 by using the arrows.

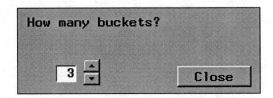

4. Select **Close** and inspect the plot that Enterprise Miner displays.

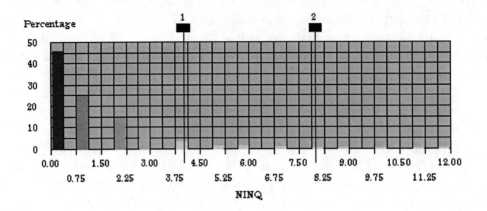

5. At the top of the window is a field for Bin and a field for Value. Bin is set to 1 by default. Type **0.5** in the Value field (for Bin 1) at the top of the window. Note: Since NINQ is a counting variable, any value larger than zero and smaller than one would yield the same split that is provided by 0.5.
6. Use the ▼ next to the field for Bin to change the selected bin from Bin 1 to Bin 2.
7. Enter **1.5** in the Value field (for Bin 2). Inspect the resulting plot.

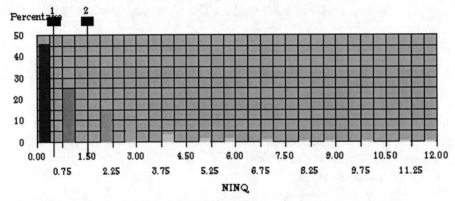

8. Close the chart to return to the Transform Variables window.

A new variable (NINQ_07W) is added to the table in this example. The new variable has the truncated name of the original variable that is followed by a random string of digits. Note that Enterprise Miner sets the value of Keep to No for the original variable. If you wanted to use both the binned variable and the original variable in the analysis, you would need to modify this attribute for NINQ and then set the value of Keep to Yes, but that is not done here. The descriptive statistics are based on metadata and your results, therefore, may vary slightly from those displayed here because of sampling variability.

Name	Keep	Formula	Mean	Std Dev	Skew
INDELINQ	Yes	DELINQ>0	0.2035	0.402702	1.47
INDEROG	Yes	DEROG>0	0.107	0.309191	2.54
LOAN	Yes		19114.25	11914.61	1.82
MORTDUE	Yes		74708.97	45846.55	1.85
VALUE	Yes		103841.4	60534.26	3.43
YOJ	No		9.071198	7.628394	0.99
YOJ_V3N0	Yes	log((YOJ + 1))	1.966028	0.910616	-0.54
DEROG	Yes		0.22919	0.813416	5.71
DELINQ	Yes		0.464444	1.172628	4.15
CLAGE	Yes		183.5176	86.60054	0.99
NINQ	No		1.189665	1.697336	2.44
NINQ_07W	Yes	NINQ	1.189665	1.697336	2.44
CLNO	Yes		21.62461	10.24814	0.74
DEBTINC	Yes		33.58185	8.09904	1.12

Examine the distribution of the new variable.

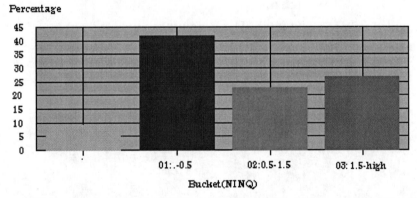

Observe that there are four histogram bars but only three bins. Observations that have a missing value for NINQ will also have a missing value for the binned version of NINQ.
Inspect the other bins. The View Info tool reveals that over 40% of the data is in the second lowest category (NINQ=0), and over 20% is in the two top categories (NINQ=1 and NINQ>2), respectively. Almost 10% of the data has missing values for NINQ.

It may be appropriate at times to keep the original variable and the created variable although that is not done here. It is uncommon to keep both variables when the original variable and the transformed variable have the same measurement level (for example, when both variables are interval). Close the node when you are finished, saving changes when you are prompted.

Understanding Data Replacement

Add a Replacement node to the Transform Variables node as shown below. The Replacement node enables you to replace missing or special values with new values. This replacement is necessary to use all of the observations in the training data for building a regression or neural network model. Decision trees handle missing values directly, while regression and neural network models ignore all observations with a missing value for any of the input variables. It is more appropriate to compare models that are built on the same set of observations. Thus, you should perform replacement before you perform any regression or neural network modeling when you plan to compare the results to those obtained from a decision tree model. Your new diagram should appear as follows:

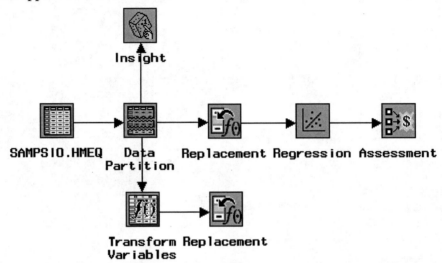

Open the newly added Replacement node. The Defaults tab is displayed first. Check the box for **Create imputed indicator variables**. The model role for these indicator variables is *rejected*. Later, you will specify *input* as the model role for some of the indicator variables, but do not do that now.

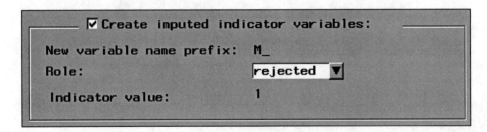

This box requests the creation of new variables, each having a prefix M_, which have a value of 1 when an observation has a missing value for the associated variable and 0 otherwise. The regression and the neural network model can use these newly created indicator variables to identify observations that had missing values before the imputation.

The Replacement node enables you to replace certain values before imputing. For example, a data set may have all missing values coded as 999. In this case, you can check the box next to

Replace before imputation; then replace the coded value by using the Constant values subtab on the Defaults tab. This is not shown here.

Using Data Replacement

Select the Data tab. Most nodes have a Data tab that enables you to see the names of the data sets that are being processed as well as a view of the data in each one. The radio button next to Training is selected. Enterprise Miner has assigned the name TRNTNVZO for the training data set and it is stored in the EMDATA library. The name of the data set is composed of some key characters (for this example, TRN) followed by several randomly generated alphanumeric characters (for this example, TNVZO).

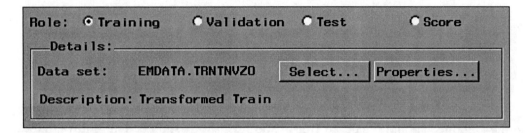

Note: SAS Release 6.12 allows only a maximum of eight alphanumeric characters for data set names. The description field enables you to identify the data set as the transformed training data. You can see the name that is assigned to the validation data set by clicking on the radio button next to Validation.

Recall that since the naming process involves random assignment, the name of your data set will almost certainly be different; however, Enterprise Miner assigns the SAS library name EMDATA to the folder that contains these files. If you create a new project, these files will be placed in a different folder, but the SAS library name will still be EMDATA. This does not cause a conflict since you can have only one project open at one time. When opening a different project, Enterprise Miner reassigns the EMDATA library name to the appropriate folder for that project.

To view a data set, select the appropriate radio button and then select **Properties**. Information about the data set appears. Select **Table View** to see the data. The training data set is shown below. Uncheck the **Variable labels** box to see the variable names.

☑ Variable labels

	BAD	LOAN	MORTDUE	VALUE	REASON	JOB
1	1	1100	25860	39025	Homelmp	Other
2	1	1500	13500	16700	Homelmp	Other
3	1	1500	.	.		
4	1	1800	28502	43034	Homelmp	Other
5	1	2000	32700	46740	Homelmp	Other

Close the Data Set Details window.

Select the **Training** subtab from the lower-right corner of the Data tab.

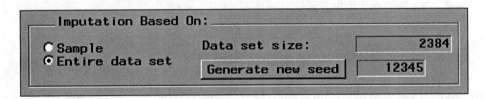

By default, the imputation is based on a random sample of the training data. The seed is used to initialize the randomization process. Generating a new seed creates a different sample. Now choose to use the entire training data set by selecting the button next to **Entire data set**. The subtab information now appears as pictured below.

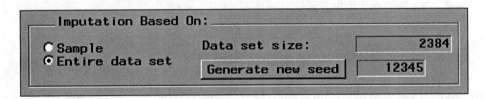

Return to the Defaults tab and select the **Imputation Methods** subtab. This shows that the default imputation method for Interval Variables is the mean (of the random sample from the training data set or of the entire training data set, depending on the settings in the Data tab). By default, imputation for class variables is done using the most frequently occurring level (or mode) in the same sample. If the most commonly occuring value is missing, Enterprise Miner uses the second most frequently occurring level in the sample.

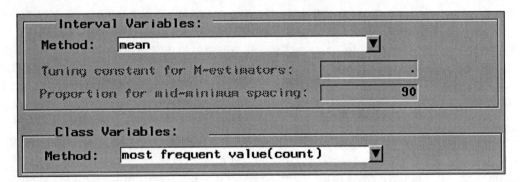

Click on the ▼ next to the method for interval variables. Enterprise Miner provides the following methods for imputing missing values for interval variables:

1. Mean - (default) or the arithmetic average
2. Median - or the 50th percentile.
3. Midrange - the maximum plus the minimum divided by two.
4. Distribution-based - replacement values are calculated based on the random percentiles of the variable's distribution.

5. Tree imputation - replacement values are estimated by using a decision tree that uses the remaining input and rejected variables that have a status of *use* in the Tree Imputation tab.
6. Tree imputation with surrogates - same as Tree inputation, but this method uses surrogate variables for splitting whenever a split variable has a missing values. In regular tree imputation, all observations that have a missing value for the split variable are placed in the same node. Surrogate splits use alternate (or surrogate) variables for splitting when the primary split variable is missing, so observations that have a missing value on the primary split variable are not necessarily placed in the same node. See the online Help for the Tree node for additional information about surrogates.
7. Mid-min spacing - the mid-minimum spacing. In calculating this statistic, the data is trimmed by using *N* percent of the data as specified in the Proportion for mid-minimum spacing field. By default, the middle 90% of the data is used to trim the original data. The maximum plus the minimum divided by two for the trimmed distribution is equal to the mid-minimum spacing.
8. Tukey's biweight, Huber's, and Andrew's wave - These are robust M-estimators of location. This class of estimators minimizes functions of the deviations of the observations from the estimate that are more general than the sum of squared deviations or the sum of absolute deviations. M-estimators generalize the idea of the maximum-likelihood estimator of the location parameter in a specified distribution.
9. Default constant - you can set a default value to be imputed for some or all variables. Instructions for using this method appear later in this section.
10. None - turns off the imputation for the interval variables.

Click on the ▼ next to the method for class variables. Enterprise Miner provides several of the same methods for imputing missing values for class variables including distribution-based, tree imputation, tree imputation with surrogates, default constant, and none. You can also select **most frequent value (count)** that uses the mode of the data that is used for imputation. If the most commonly occurring value for a variable is missing, Enterprise Miner uses the next most frequently occurring value.

Select **Tree imputation** as the imputation method for both types of variables.

This tab sets the default imputation method for each type of variable. You will later see how to change the imputation method for a variable. When you are using tree imputation for imputing missing values, use the entire training data set for more consistent results.

Select the **Constant values** subtab of the Defaults tab. This subtab enables you to replace certain values (before imputing, if you want, by using the checkbox on the General subtab of the Defaults tab). It also enables you to specify constants for imputing missing values. Type **0** in the imputation field for numeric variables and Unknown in the imputation field for character variables.

```
┌─Trimming of Interval Variables:──────────────────────────┐
│  Replace <:  [            ] .    With value (<): [        ] . │
│                                                              │
│  Replace >:  [            ] .    With value (>): [        ] . │
├─Imputation:──────────────────────────────────────────────┤
│  Numeric variables:   [              0] │
│  Character variables: [Unknown                            ] │
└──────────────────────────────────────────────────────────┘
```

The constants that are specified in this tab are used to impute the missing values for a variable when you select default constant as the imputation method. This example uses tree imputation as the default imputation method; however, a later example modifies the imputation method for some of the variables to use the default constant that is specified here.

Select the **Tree Imputation** tab. This tab enables you to set the variables that will be used for tree imputation.

Inputs for tree imputation:

Name	Status	Model Role	Measurement	Type
LOAN	use	input	interval	num
MORTDUE	use	input	interval	num
VALUE	use	input	interval	num
DEROG	use	input	interval	num
DELINQ	use	input	interval	num
CLAGE	use	input	interval	num
CLNO	use	input	interval	num
DEBTINC	use	input	interval	num
INDELINQ	use	input	interval	num
INDEROG	use	input	interval	num
YOJ_V3N0	use	input	interval	num
REASON	use	input	binary	char
JOB	use	input	nominal	char
NINQ_07W	use	input	ordinal	num

Note that the target variable (BAD) is not available, and rejected variables have Status set to *don't use* by default. To use a rejected variable, you can set the Status to *use* by positioning the tip of your cursor on the row of the desired variable and then clicking on **Set Status → use**. However, none of the variables in the data set have been rejected, so this is not a consideration for this example.

Select the **Interval Variables** tab.

Suppose you want to change the imputation method for VALUE to mean. To do so, proceed as follows:

1. Position the tip of your cursor on the row for VALUE in the Imputation Method column and right-click.
2. Select **Select Method → Mean**.

Suppose you want to change the imputed value for DEROG and DELINQ to zero. Although zero is the default constant, you can practice setting up this imputed value by using different methods. Use Default Constant to impute the values for DEROG, but use Set Value to specify the imputed value for DELINQ. To change the imputation method for DEROG, proceed as follows:

1. Position the tip of your cursor on the row for DEROG in the Imputation Method column and right-click.
2. Select **Select Method → default constant**.

Now set the imputation method for DELINQ. To do so, proceed as follows:

1. Position the tip of your cursor on the row for DELINQ in the Imputation Method column and right-click.
2. Select **Select Method → set Value**.
3. Type **0** in the **New Value** field.
4. Select **OK**.

A portion of the window appears below.

Name	Status	Model Role	Imputation Method
LOAN	use	input	tree imputation
MORTDUE	use	input	tree imputation
VALUE	use	input	mean
DEROG	use	input	default constant - 0
DELINQ	use	input	set value - 0
CLAGE	use	input	tree imputation
CLNO	use	input	tree imputation
DEBTINC	use	input	tree imputation
INDELINQ	use	input	tree imputation
INDEROG	use	input	tree imputation
YOJ_V3N0	use	input	tree imputation

Even though you specified the imputation in different ways, the imputed value for DEROG and DELINQ will be the same. Were you to change the default constant value, however, it would affect the imputation for DEROG but not for DELINQ.

Select the **Class Variables** tab. Observe that the Status of BAD is set to *don't use*, which indicates that the missing values for this variable will not be replaced.

Name	Status	Imputation Method	Replace Value
BAD	don't use	tree imputation	
REASON	use	tree imputation	
JOB	use	tree imputation	
NINQ_07W	use	tree imputation	

Suppose that you want to use Unknown (the default constant) as the imputed value for REASON, and you want to use Other as the imputed value for JOB.

To modify the imputation method for REASON, proceed as follows:
1. Right-click on the row for REASON in the Imputation Method column.
2. Select **Select method → default constant**.

To modify the imputation method for JOB, proceed as follows:
3. Right-click on the row for JOB in the Imputation Method column.
4. Select **Select method → set value**.

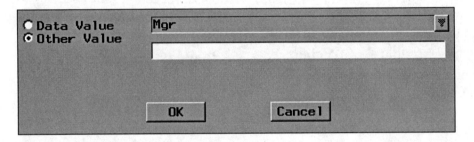

5. Select the radio button next to **Data Value**.
6. Use the ▼ to select Other from the list of data values.

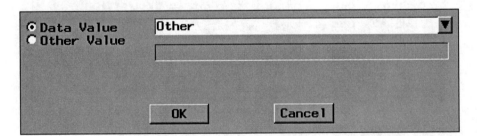

7. Select **OK** to accept the value.

Inspect the resulting window. Your settings should match those shown below.

Name	Status	Imputation Method
BAD	don't use	tree imputation
REASON	use	default constant - Unknown
JOB	use	set value - Other
NINQ_07W	use	tree imputation

Select the **Output** tab. While the Data tab shows the input data, the Output tab shows the output data set information.

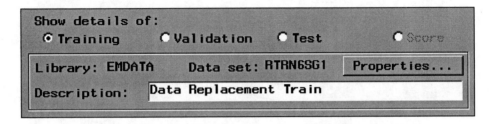

Close the Replacement node and save the changes when you are prompted.

2.4 Fitting and Comparing Candidate Models

Fitting a Regression Model

Add a new Regression node to the workspace and connect it to the recently modified Replacement node. Then connect the Regression node to the Assessment node. Compare your flow to the one below.

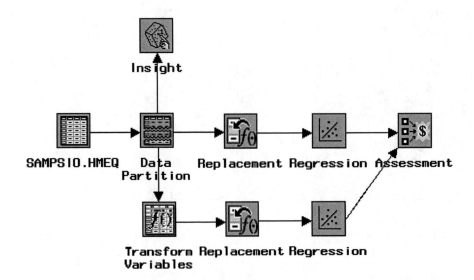

Open the Regression node that you just added to the workspace. Find the Tools menu on the top of the session window and select **Tools → Interaction Builder**. The Interaction Builder enables you to easily add interactions and higher-order terms to the model, although that is not shown now.   A portion of this tool is shown below.

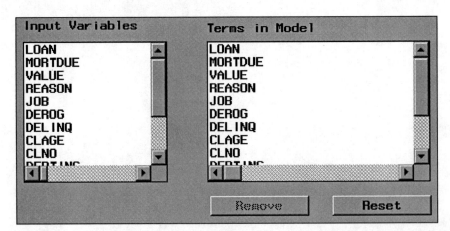

The input variables are shown on the left, while the effects in the model are shown on the right. The Regression node fits a model that contains all main effects by default. Close the Interaction Builder window without making any changes.

Select the **Selection Method** tab. This tab enables you to perform different types of variable selection by using various criteria. No variable selection is done by default.

You can choose from the following variable selection techniques:
1. Backward - begins, by default, with all candidate effects in the model and then systematically removes effects that are not significantly associated with the target until no other effect in the model meets the Stay Significance Level or until the Stop criterion is met. This method is not recommended for binary or ordinal targets when there are many candidate effects or when there are many levels for some classification input variables.
2. Forward - begins, by default, with no candidate effects in the model and then systematically adds effects that are significantly associated with the target until none of the remaining effects meet the Entry Significance Level or until the Stop criterion is met.
3. Stepwise - As in the Forward method, Stepwise selection begins, by default, with no candidate effects in the model and then systematically adds effects that are significantly associated with the target. However, after an effect is added to the model, Stepwise may remove any effect that is already in the model, but that is not significantly associated with the target.
4. None - (default) all candidate effects are included in the final model.

Choose Stepwise by using the next to the Method field.

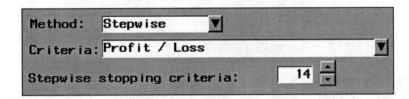

The stopping criteria field enables you to set the maximum number of steps before the Stepwise method stops. The default is set to the number of effects in the model.

The Stepwise method uses cutoffs for variables to enter the model and for variables to leave the model.

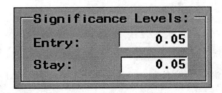

Changing these values may affect the final variables that are included in the model. No changes are necessary for the purposes of this example.

Inspect the Effect Hierarchy options in the lower-left corner of the Selection Method tab.

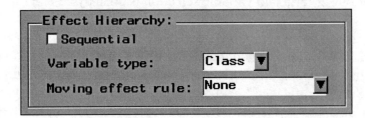

Model hierarchy refers to the requirement that for any effect in the model, all effects that it contains must also be in the model. For example, in order for the interaction A*B to be in the model, the main effects A and B must also be in the model. The Effect Hierarchy options enable you to control how a set of effects is entered into or removed from the model during the effect-selection process. No changes are necessary for the purposes of this example.

Consider the Number of Variables subsection in the lower-right corner of the window.

This subsection enables you to select a specified number of effects to begin the selection process (for forward) or select a minimum number of effects to remain in the model. The order depends on the order that is displayed in the Interaction Profiler. To change the order of effects, you can select **Tools → Model Ordering**, but no ordering is done for this example.

Close the Regression node and save the changes when you are prompted. Since you have changed the default settings for the node, it prompts you to change the default model name. Type **StepReg** in the Model Name field.

Select **OK**.

Evaluating the Model

Right-click on the Assessment node and select **Run**. This enables you to generate and compare lift charts for the two regression models. Observe that each node becomes green as it runs. Since you ran the flow from the Assessment node, you are prompted to see the Assessment results. Select **Yes** to see these results. Inspect the table that appears.
If you scroll the window to the right, Enterprise Miner displays several typical regression statistics such as asymptotic standard error (ASE).

Tool	Model ID	Name	Description	Target	Target Event
Regression	_A0000B9	StepReg		BAD	1
Regression	_A00008G	Untitled		BAD	1

Since more than one Regression node is connected to the Assessment node, you need to use the model name to identify which regression came from the default regression model and which one came from the stepwise regression model. Observe that one line has the name `StepReg` but the other line has the name `Untitled`. Rename the model that is currently named `Untitled` to `DefReg` since it represents the default regression model that uses the default data imputation. Press the ENTER key to enter the new name before you proceed. Highlight both rows and then select **Tools → Lift Chart**.

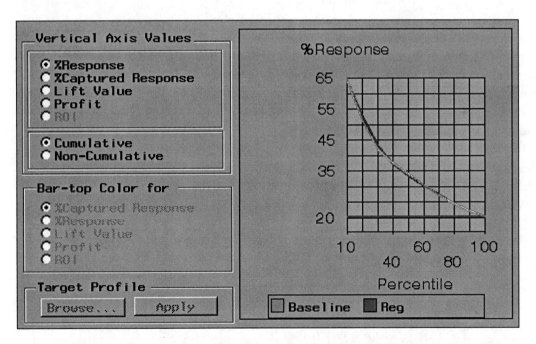

A Cumulative %Response chart is shown by default. You can see which line belongs to which model by selecting **Format → Model Name**, but that is not shown here. Recall that this chart groups individuals based on the predicted probability of response, and then plots the percentage of respondents. The two lines are almost indistinguishable in this case. You will learn later how to obtain additional results on each model. When doing so, you will find that the stepwise regression model included all variables except YOJ and REASON.

Fitting a Default Decision Tree

To add a default Tree node to the workspace, connect the Data Partition to the Tree, and then connect the Tree to the Assessment node. The flow should now appear like the one pictured below. This section explains why the tree is connected to the Data Partition node and not to the Replacement node.

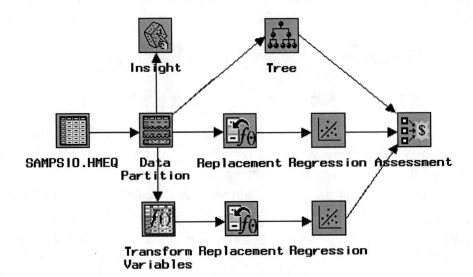

The reason is that a decision tree handles missing values directly, so it does not need data replacement. Monotonic transformations of interval numeric variables will probably not improve the tree fit since the tree groups numeric variables into bins. In fact, the tree may actually perform worse if you connect it after grouping a variable into bins in the Transform Variables node, since the bins reduce the splits that the tree can consider (unless you include the original variable and the grouped variable in the model).

Run the flow from the Assessment node and select **Yes** when you are prompted to view the results. Nodes that have been executed previously are not run again. The Assessment node opens with three models displayed.

Type the name **DefTree** in the Name column for the Tree tool to indicate that you have fit a default tree. Your window should now look like the one below.

Tool	Model ID	Name	Description	Target	Target Event
Tree	_A0000GV	DefTree		BAD	1
Regression	_A000008G	DefReg		BAD	1
Regression	_A0000E2	StepReg		BAD	1

Your models may appear in different order depending on the sequence in which you connected and ran each of the nodes. The Model ID column also contains different values. The Model ID is used by Enterprise Miner to distinguish among the models. None of these potential naming or order differences has any impact on the results.

To generate a lift chart, highlight all rows in the Assessment node. You can do this by selecting the row for one model and then CTRL-clicking on the rows for the other models. You can also drag through all of the rows to highlight them simultaneously. Your resulting window should appear like the diagram below.

Tool	Model ID	Name	Description	Target	Target Event
Tree	_A0000GV	DefTree		BAD	1
Regression	_A00008G	DefReg		BAD	1
Regression	_A0000E2	StepReg		BAD	1

The lift chart that you will construct is based on the validation data set. To verify that the validation data set is being used, inspect the Tools menu and observe the checkmark next to Validation Data Set. Enterprise Miner does not compute assessment information for all data sets by default, so not all charts are available on all data sets. Select **Tools → Lift Chart** to compare how the models perform on the validation data set. Observe that the tree model outperforms both regression models.

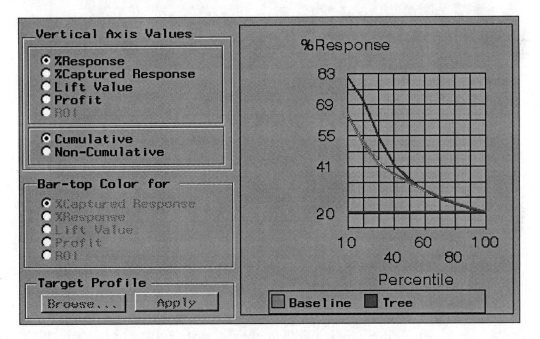

Occasionally the entire legend is not visible. You can often see the entire legend by maximizing the window. Otherwise, it may be necessary to modify the graph window.

To modify the graph window,

- click on the **Move/Reside Legend** icon ( ) on the toolbar at the top to move or resize the legend. Click on a side of the legend box to resize (cursor appears as a double-sided arrow). Click in the middle to move the legend (cursor appears as a hand). Dragging resizes or moves the legend, depending on the cursor appearance.

The resized legend appears below.

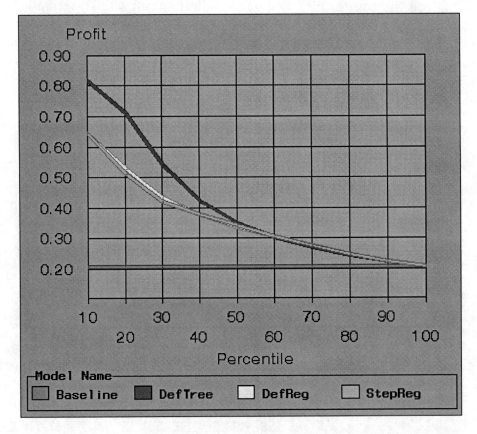

- click on the **Move Graph** icon ( ) on the toolbar and reposition the graph.

The default legend and formatted legend are pictured below. To use the names that you typed, select **Format → Model Name** from the menu at the top of the window. Inspect the plot and observe that the default tree seems to greatly outperform both the of the regression models.

One possible reason for the difference could lie in the fact that decision trees are highly flexible modeling techniques. Regression models, by comparison, are relatively inflexible unless you add additional terms such as interactions or polynomial effects. Another reason could be the way in which decision trees handle missing values. Recall that you had to impute missing values before building a regression model on all of the training data, while decision trees can handle missing values without imputation.

To evaluate the extent of the difference which may be attributable to the inflexibility of the regression model, consider fitting a neural network model. Although neural networks require complete observations (just like regression models), they are extremely flexible.
Close the Assessment node when you have finished inspecting the various lift charts.

Fitting a Default Neural Network

Add a default Neural Network node to the workspace. Connect the most recently added Replacement node to the Neural Network, and then connect the Neural Network node to the Assessment node. The flow should now appear like the one pictured below.

Note: A monitor appears when the neural network is executed. This monitor allows you to stop the neural network at any time. If the monitor does not show any activity for a few moments, select **Stop** and then **Continue** on the monitor to restart the process. The monitor may not appear when you run in client/server mode, depending on your machine settings.

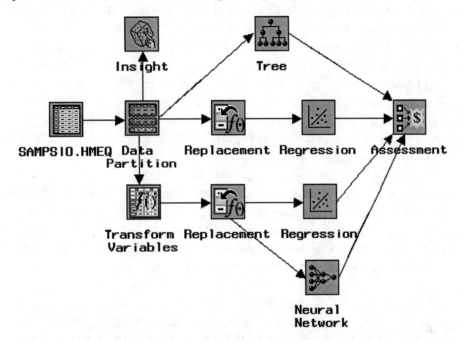

Run the flow from the Assessment node. Select **Yes** when you are prompted to view the results. Rename the neural network from Untitled to DefNN. Highlight all four models and select **Tools → Lift Chart** to compare these models.

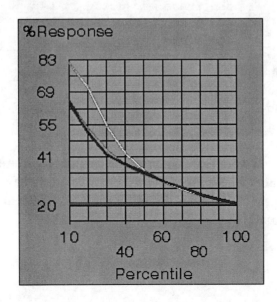

Investigating the Regression and Neural Network Models

The default neural network does not perform any better than the regression model. If both models perform poorly compared to the decision tree, it may be due to how missing values are handled. The tree will handle observations with missing values, while the regression and neural network models will ignore observations with missing values.

To handle the missing values, you added an imputation node so that all of the observations would be used for building and evaluating the model. The effect of this replacement, however, is that you replace a missing value (perhaps an unusual value for the variable) with an imputed value (a typical value for the variable). Imputation can therefore change an observation from being somewhat unusual with respect to a particular variable to very typical with respect to that variable. For example, if someone were applying for a loan and had a missing value for INCOME, the Replacement node (by default) would replace that value with the mean for INCOME in a sample from the training data. In practice, someone who has an average value for INCOME would often be evaluated differently from someone who has a missing value for INCOME on a loan application; however, the regression and neural network models could not distinguish between these two cases.

One solution to this problem is to create missing value indicators to indicate if an observation originally had a missing value before imputation was performed. The missing value indicators allow the regression and neural network models to differentiate between observations that originally had missing values and those observations with non-missing values. The addition of missing value indicators can greatly improve a neural network or regression model.

Recall that you checked the box to add these indicators in the last Replacement node. To find out what happened to these indicators, open the most recently edited Regression node. The Variables tab is active. Scroll to the bottom of the tab. A portion of the output is shown below.

Name	Status	Model Role	Measurement
M_CLNO	don't use	rejected	binary
M_DEBTIN	don't use	rejected	binary
M_INDELI	don't use	rejected	unary
M_INDERO	don't use	rejected	unary
M_YOJ_V3	don't use	rejected	binary
M_REASON	don't use	rejected	binary
M_JOB	don't use	rejected	binary
M_NINQ_0	don't use	rejected	binary

Specify the indicators that you want to consider in your model by setting their status to *use*. Those missing value indicators whose measurement level is unary have only one level and that implies that the corresponding variable has no missing values (or all missing values). Therefore, these missing value indicators will not be useful in the model.

Previous investigation has determined that a missing value for DEBTINC is strongly related to the target; therefore, change the status of M_DEBTIN (the missing value indicator for DEBTINC) to **use** and rerun the regression model.

Name	Status	Model Role	Measurement
M_CLNO	don't use	rejected	binary
M_DEBTIN	use	rejected	binary
M_INDELI	don't use	rejected	unary

Close the Regression node, saving changes when you are prompted. Rerun the flow from the Assessment node, and view the results when you are prompted. Build a lift chart for the decision tree (DefTree) and the new regression model (StepReg). Investigate whether adding the missing value indicator variable has made a difference.

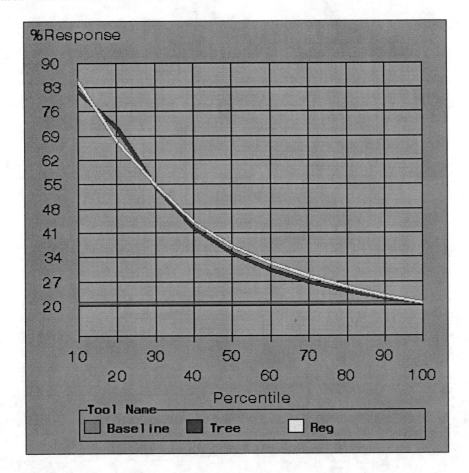

Now the regression model outperforms the tree in the first decile. Both models have very similar performance on the validation data set. This example illustrates that missing variables can have a dramatic impact on performance.

In general, it is impossible to know whether a decision tree, a regression model, or a neural network model will provide the best results. For this data (or for any other), a good analyst will consider many variations of each model and identify the best one according to his or her criteria. In this case, assume that the regression model is selected.

2.5 Generating and Using Scoring Code

After deciding on a model, you will often need to be able to use your model to score new or existing observations. The Score node can be used to evaluate, save, and combine scoring code from different models. In this example, you want to score a data set by using the regression model.

Modify your workspace to appear like the diagram below as follows:
1. Drag a Score node onto the workspace and position it below the Assessment node.
2. Connect the Regression node to the Score node.

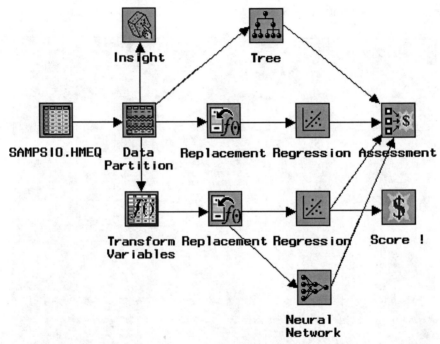

Open the Score node. The Settings tab is active. The Settings tab provides options for you when you run the Score node in a path.

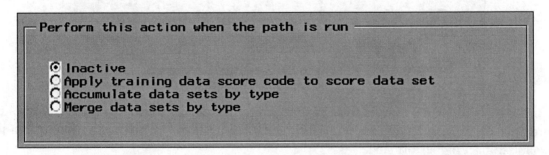

By default, no action is taken. The Score node collects scoring code, but it does not modify any data sets unless you change the settings on this tab. Do not change the settings now.

```
┌─Perform this action when the path is run ────────────────────┐
│                                                              │
│  ◉ Inactive                                                  │
│  ○ Apply training data score code to score data set          │
│  ○ Accumulate data sets by type                              │
│  ○ Merge data sets by type                                   │
│                                                              │
└──────────────────────────────────────────────────────────────┘
```

The following radio button choices are available on the Settings tab:
1. Inactive (default) - exports the most recently created scored data sets.
2. Apply training data score code to score data set - applies scoring code to the score data set.
3. Accumulate data sets by type - copies and exports data sets that are imported from predecessor nodes. If you use this action in a path that contains a group processing node, the output data sets are concatenated.
4. Merge data sets by type - merges data sets that are imported from predecessor nodes. For example, you can use this action to merge the training data sets from two modeling nodes to compare the predicted values.

The Score Code tab enables you to see the scoring code for each modeling node that is connected to the Score node. Only the Regression node is connected to the Score node, so you see only scoring code for the regression model.

```
┌─────────────────────────────────────┐ ▼ │
│ Current Imports                       │   │
└───────────────────────────────────────────┘

┌──────────────────────────┐  ┌────────────────────────────────────┐
│ Regression - T1RKGHZR     │  │ 00001 *;                            │
│                           │  │ 00002 /*START_CHUNK 1251885140.2 */ │
│                           │  │ 00003 *;                            │
│                           │  │ 00004 * NODE: Data Partition ;      │
│                           │  │ 00005 * TIME: 02SEP99:09:52:20 ;    │
│                           │  │ 00006 *;                            │
└──────────────────────────┘  └────────────────────────────────────┘
```

Click on the ▼ to see the available management functions. By default, the Current Imports are listed in the left list box of the Score code tab. The other list options include
- Current imports - (default) lists the scoring code that is currently imported from node predecessors.
- Accumulated runs - lists the scoring code that is exported by the node's predecessors during the most recent path run (training action). If the training action involves group processing, a separate score entry is listed for each group iteration for each predecessor node. This is the only access to score code that is generated from group processing.
- Saved - lists saved or merged score code entries.
- All - lists all score code entries that are managed by the node.

To see the scoring code for a model, double-click on the desired model in the list on the left, and the associated scoring code is displayed in the window on the right.
The scoring code is a SAS program that performs a SAS data step. You can use the scoring code on any system that runs base SAS software. If you modify the settings in a modeling node and run the flow, the scoring code that is associated with the affected model is updated.

To keep modifications in the workspace from affecting the scoring code, you can save the scoring code as follows:
1. Select the name of the model that was used for developing the scoring code that you want to save from the list on the left-hand side of the window. For this example, save the scoring code for the regression model.
2. Right-click on the selected model and select **Save**.

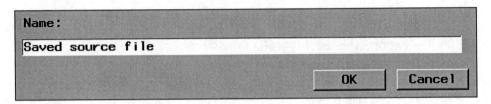

A dialog box opens that enables you to name the saved source file. You can type a name if you want, although this is not necessary.

3. Type in a name, such as **My Regression Code**.

4. Press **OK**. Note the change in the management function from Current Imports to Saved.

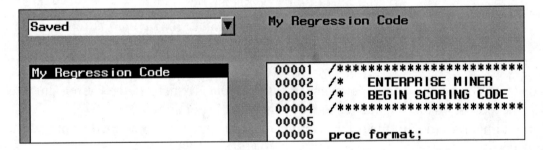

The code is now saved within Enterprise Miner. To use the code outside Enterprise Miner in a SAS session, you need to export the scoring code from Enterprise Miner as follows:
1. Highlight the name that represents the desired code in the list on the left side.
2. Right-click on the highlighted name and select **Export**.
3. Type a name for the saved program such as **MYCODE** and select **Save**.

Scoring Using Base SAS

You can use the saved scoring code to score a data set by using base SAS. The program requires base SAS only to run; therefore, you can run the program on any of the systems in which you have installed base SAS whether or not Enterprise Miner is installed.

Enterprise Miner runs on top of a SAS session, and you can use this SAS session at any time. Use this SAS session to score the DMAHMEQ data set in the SAMPSIO library. This is a data set with all of the inputs for the model. This data set also has response information so that you can compare the predicted outcome to the actual outcome if you want.

To score the data set using SAS, proceed as follows:
1. Select **Window → Program Editor** to make the SAS session active.
2. Select **File → Open**.
3. Find and select the program that you just saved (named MYCODE in this example). Note: If you used the default folder when you save the code, it will be in the same folder that opens when you select **File → Open**.
4. Select **Open**. The scoring code appears in the Program Editor of the SAS session. A portion of the code appears below.

```
/*************************************************/
/*    ENTERPRISE MINER                           */
/*    BEGIN SCORING CODE                         */
/*************************************************/

proc format;
value NINQ_07_
low-0.5='01:.-0.5'
0.5-1.5='02:0.5-1.5'
1.5-high='03:1.5-high'
:
;
;
%macro DMNORLEN; 16 %mend DMNORLEN;

%macro DMNORMCP(in,out);
&out=substr(left(&in),1,min(%dmnorlen,length(left(&in))));
&out=upcase(&out);
%mend DMNORMCP;

%macro DMNORMIP(in);
&in=left(&in);
&in=substr(&in,1,min(%dmnorlen,length(&in)));
&in=upcase(&in);
%mend DMNORMIP;


DATA &_PREDICT ; SET &_SCORE ;
```

The data set _PREDICT contains the predicted values. The data set represented by _SCORE is the data set that you want to score. Since these data sets are being used in a macro (preceded by "&_"), the data sets need to be initialized.

5. Score the DMAHMEQ data set in the SAMPSIO library. To do so, first initialize _PREDICT and _SCORE by placing the following code before the beginning of the scoring code that you opened in step 4 :

```
%let _SCORE=SAMPSIO.DMAHMEQ;
%let _PREDICT=X;
```

The second line will initialize _PREDICT. There is actually no X data set. It is just a dummy name. The actual _PREDICT data set is re-created by the scoring code.

6. To see the results of scoring, add the following code at the end of the scoring code that you opened in step 4:

```
PROC PRINT DATA=&_PREDICT;
VAR BAD P_BAD1 P_BAD0;
RUN;
```

This code prints the value of BAD as well as P_BAD1 (predicted probability BAD=1) and P_BAD0 (predicted probability BAD=0).

Optional: Although it is unnecessary, you may want to sort the observations according to one of the variables, say, P_BAD1. To do so, submit the following code before submitting the PROC PRINT code that was given above.

```
PROC SORT DATA=&_PREDICT;
BY DESCENDING P_BAD1;
RUN;
```

By sorting the observations by descending values of P_BAD1, you arrange the top observations to be those that are most likely to default.

7. Submit the scoring code by selecting **Locals → Submit** or by selecing the **Submit** icon (🏃) from the toolbar. Inspect the resulting output (the first 10 observations of the newly sorted data set are shown below).

OBS	BAD	P_BAD1	P_BAD0
1	1	0.99997	0.000029
2	1	0.99995	0.000051
3	1	0.99955	0.000446
4	1	0.99949	0.000507
5	1	0.99940	0.000599
6	1	0.99935	0.000650
7	1	0.99931	0.000687
8	1	0.99862	0.001376
9	1	0.99857	0.001426
10	1	0.99821	0.001789

Observe that since BAD has two levels (0 and 1), that P_BAD1+P_BAD0=1. All of the first ten observations represent defaulters, as may have been expected from the high probability of default (shown in P_BAD1).

8. Select **Window → Score!** to return to Enterprise Miner.
9. Close the Score node to return to the Enterprise Miner workspace.

Scoring within Enterprise Miner

You have just used the saved scoring code to score a data set by using base SAS. Now score the same data set by using Enterprise Miner. Begin by adding another Input Data Source node to the flow and connect it to the Score node. Add an Insight node and connect the Score node to it as pictured below.

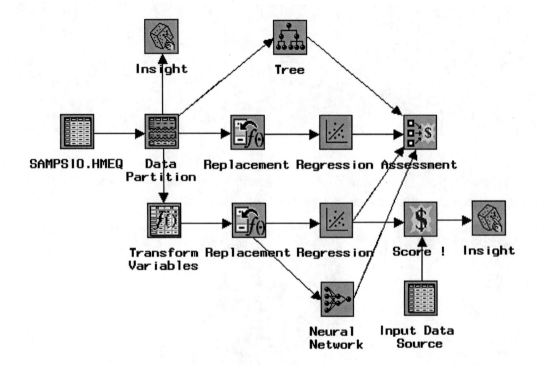

Select the DMAHMEQ data set from SAMPSIO library.

Change the role of the data set from RAW to SCORE.

Observe that the data set has 5,960 rows and 13 columns.

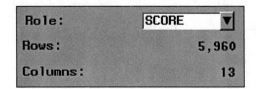

Inspect the variables if you want. There is no need to modify the variables here, since the role and level of each variable is built into the scoring code. After inspection, close this Input Data Source, and save changes when you are prompted.

Open the Score node. By default the Score node is inactive when you are running items in a path. Select the radio button next to **Apply training data score code to score data set**. The Score node now adds prediction information to the data set that it is scoring.

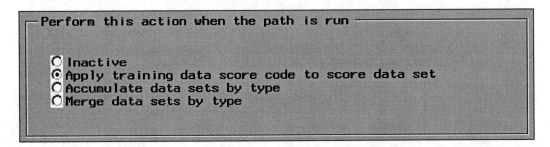

After requesting the Score node to apply the scoring data, the Output variables subtab becomes available. This subtab enables you to control what values are added to the scored data set. Select the **Output variables** subtab and inspect the window that is displayed.

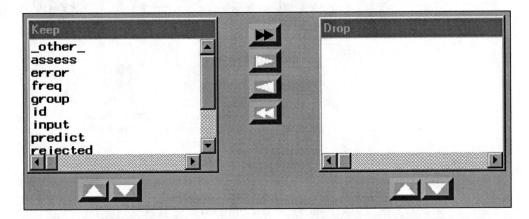

All variables are included by default, but the options that are shown below enable you to drop certain variables if you want. Dropped variables are excluded from the output data set. No variables are dropped in this example.

Close the Score node, saving changes when you are prompted.

Next open the Insight node. Choose the Select option on the Data tab to select the data set to be associated with the score data. This data set typically has an SD prefix followed by a string of random alphanumeric characters.

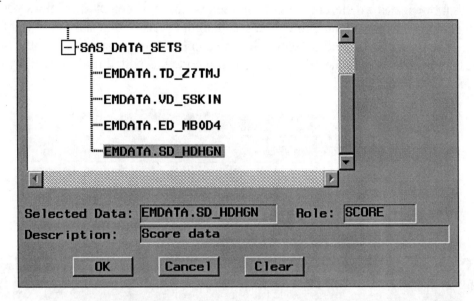

The selected data set is SD_HDHGN in this example, although the name of your data set will be different. The Description field indicates that this data set represents score data.

Select **OK** to return to the Data tab in Insight. Then close Insight, saving changes when you are prompted. Run Insight and view the results.

The scored data set now has 39 variables. Only 13 variables were in the original data set, so the scoring code has added 26 additional variables to this data set. If you only want to add selected variables when scoring, you can specify fewer variables in the Score node as described earlier. The data set that opens has a different name from the one that you selected. Unless you select the option to perform Insight on the entire data set, Insight opens with a sample of 2,000 observations. The prefix SMP_ indicates that it is a sample. You can see some of the newly created variables by scrolling to the right. The scoring code has added missing value indicators as well as prediction information.

EMPROJ.SMP_SDTA

39	Int	Int	Int	Int	Nom	Nom
2000	BAD	LOAN	MORTDUE	VALUE	REASON	JOB
1	1	1500	70189.605	102554.69	Unknown	Other
2	0	1700	97800.000	112000.00	Home Imp	Office
3	1	1800	48649.000	57037.00	Home Imp	Other
4	1	2000	20627.000	29800.00	Home Imp	Office
5	1	2000	45000.000	55000.00	Home Imp	Other

EMPROJ.SMP_SDTA

39	Int	Nom	Nom	Int	Int	Int
2000	M_NINQ_0	F_BAD	I_BAD	R_BAD1	R_BAD0	P_BAD1
1	1	1	0	0.57404	-0.57404	0.42596
2	0	0	0	-0.43844	0.43844	0.43844
3	0	1	1	0.02557	-0.02557	0.97443
4	0	1	0	0.56783	-0.56783	0.43217
5	0	1	1	0.40794	-0.40794	0.59206

2.6 Generating a Report Using the Reporter Node

To create an HTML report, you can add a Reporter node to your workspace. Add the reporter node after the Assessment node so that the Assessment results are included in the report. Run the flow from the Reporter node. Observe that the nodes become green as the flow is checked, and the nodes become yellow as the report is generated.

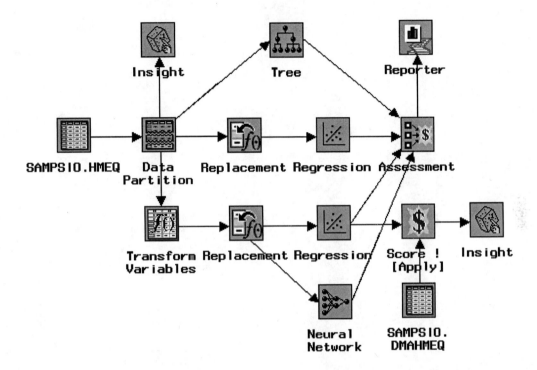

When the run is finished, you can select **OK** to acknowledge the creation of the HTML report or **Open** to open the report and view it with your default Internet browser.

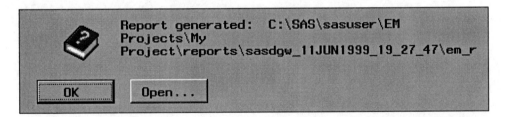

If you do not look at the report, you can view it later by selecting the **Reports** subtab. The HTML report contains the results from each node in any path that leads to the Reporter. Some of the results are in the main document, while others are accessible through hyperlinks from the main document. All files that are associated with a report are placed in a folder that is located in the reports folder of the corresponding project folder. The path to the reports folder is shown in the dialog box that is displayed after the report is generated. For example, the dialog box above indicates that the report is located in C:\SAS\sasuser\EM Projects\My Project\reports\ sasdgw_11JUN1999_19_27_47, and the main document file is em_report.html (the complete filename is not displayed).

Chapter 3: Variable Selection

3.1 Introduction to Variable Selection

Data often contains an extremely large number of variables. Using all of the variables in a model is not practical in general, so variable selection plays a critical role in modeling. The previous chapter used stepwise regression to perform variable selection; however, this method may not perform well when you are evaluating data sets that contain hundreds of potential input variables. Furthermore, the stepwise selection method is available only in the Regression node. Variable selection is often more critical for the Neural Network node because of the large number of parameters that are generated in relation to using the same number of variables in a regression model.

Since variable selection is a critical phase in model building, Enterprise Miner provides selection methods in two nodes, the Tree node and the Variable Selection node. Variables that are selected by either of these two nodes are immediately available to any subsequent modeling node, including the Regression node. No single method of selecting variables for use in another modeling tool is uniformly best. It is often useful to consider many types of variable selection in evaluating the importance of each variable.

This chapter demonstrates how to identify important variables by using the Variable Selection node. Although you can also perform variable selection by using the Decision Tree node, that method is not covered here. For convenience, consider the first flow that you constructed. Add a Variable Selection node after the Replacement node that is connected to the Transform Variables node. Your workspace should now appear as follows:

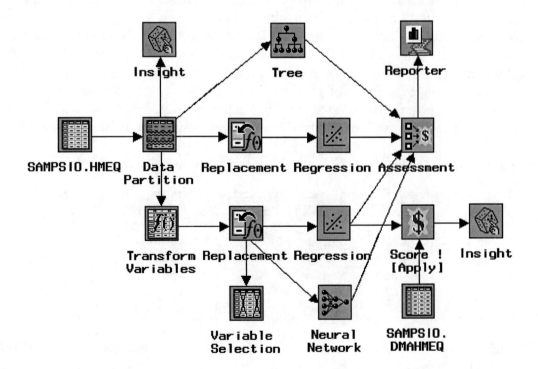

3.2 Using the Variable Selection Node

Open the Variable Selection node. The Variables tab is active. A portion of the window is displayed below. Scroll down to see the missing value indicator variables.

Name	Status	Model Role	Measurement
BAD	use	target	binary
LOAN	use	input	interval
MORTDUE	use	input	interval
VALUE	use	input	interval
REASON	use	input	nominal
JOB	use	input	nominal
DEROG	use	input	interval
DELINQ	use	input	interval
CLAGE	use	input	interval
CLNO	use	input	interval
DEBTINC	use	input	interval
INDELINQ	use	input	interval
INDEROG	use	input	interval
YOJ_V3N0	use	input	interval
NINQ_07W	use	input	ordinal
M_LOAN	don't use	rejected	unary
M_MORTDU	don't use	rejected	binary

Observe that the missing value indicators have *rejected* listed for Model Role; these indicators are rejected by default, and therefore their Status is set to *don't use*. If you want to identify which (if any) of the missing value indicators would be useful in prediction, you must change their Status to *use*. The missing value indicators with a *unary* measurement level will not be useful since *unary* indicates that every observation in the data set has the same value. Change the Status of all of the missing indicator variables to *use*. Variables with the *unary* measurement level are dropped automatically. Note: You will not see the missing value indicator variables unless you have previously run the Replacement node.

Select the Manual Selection tab. A portion of the window is displayed below.

Name	Measurement	Role Assignment
DEBTINC	interval	<automatic>
INDELINQ	interval	<automatic>
INDEROG	interval	<automatic>
YOJ_V3N0	interval	<automatic>
NINQ_07W	ordinal	<automatic>
M_LOAN	unary	<automatic>

This tab enables you to force variables to be included or excluded from future analyses. By default, the role assignment is automatic, which means that the role is set based on the analysis performed in this node. All variables whose Status was set to *use* appear in this tab. If you want to ensure that a variable is included, specify the Role Assignment as *input*.

Selection Using R-square Criterion

Select the Target Associations tab. This tab enables you to choose one of two selection criteria and specify options for the chosen criterion. By default, the node removes variables that are unrelated to the target (according to the settings that are used for the selection criterion) and scores the data sets. Consider the settings that are associated with the default R-square criterion first.

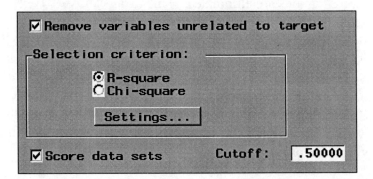

Since R-square is already selected as the selection criterion, click on the **Settings** button on the Target Association tab.

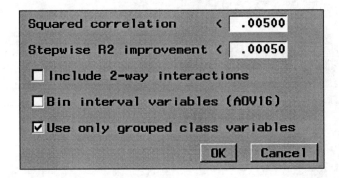

The R-square criterion uses a goodness-of-fit criterion to evaluate variables. It uses a stepwise method of selecting variables that stops when the improvement in the R2 is less than 0.00050. By default, the method rejects variables whose contribution is less than 0.005.

The following three-step process is done when you apply the R-square variable selection criterion to a binary target. If the target is nonbinary, only the first two steps are performed.

1. Enterprise Miner computes the squared correlation (R^2) for each variable with the target and then assigns the rejected role to those variables that have a value less than the Squared correlation criterion (default 0.00500).
2. Enterprise Miner evaluates the remaining significant (chosen) variables by using a forward stepwise R^2 regression. Variables that have a stepwise R^2 improvement less than the threshold criterion (default 0.00050) are assigned the rejected role.
3. For binary targets, Enterprise Miner performs a logistic regression by using the predicted values that are output from the forward stepwise regression as the independent input variable.

Additional options on the Settings tab enable you to
- test 2-way interactions - when selected, this option requests Enterprise Miner to create and evaluate 2-way interactions for categorical inputs.
- group interval variables in up to 16 bins - when selected, this option requests Enterprise Miner to bin interval variables into 16 equally spaced groups (AOV16) . The AOV16 variables are created to help identify nonlinear relationships with the target. Bins that contain zero observations are eliminated. This means an AOV16 variable can have fewer than 16 bins.
- use only grouped class variables - when this is selected, Enterprise Miner uses only the grouped class variable to evaluate variable importance. A grouped class variable may or may not have fewer levels than the original class variables. To create the grouped variable, Enterprise Miner attempts to combine levels of the variable with similar behavior. Deselecting this option requests Enterprise Miner to use the grouped class variable as well as the original class variable in evaluating variable importance, which may greatly increase processing time.

Leave the default settings and close the node. Run the flow from the Variable Selection node and view the results. The Variables tab is active. To see the results more easily, click on the **Role** column heading. Then click on the **Rejection Reason** column heading to sort by rejection reason. Inspect the results.

Name	Role	Rejection Reason
DEROG	input	
DELINQ	input	
CLAGE	input	
DEBTINC	input	
G_JOB	input	
M_VALUE	rejected	
M_DEROG	rejected	
M_DEBTIN	rejected	
JOB	rejected	Group variable G_JOB preferred
LOAN	rejected	Low R2 w/ target
MORTDUE	rejected	Low R2 w/ target

Observe that DEROG, DELINQ, CLAGE, DEBTINC, G_JOB, M_VALUE, M_DEROG, and M_DEBTIN are retained. Note that G_JOB is the grouped version of the JOB variable, while the variables that have the M_ prefix are the missing value indicators for VALUE, DEROG, and DEBTINC, respectively. The role of M_VALUE, M_DEROG, and M_DEBTIN are set to *rejected* since this was the default for missing value indicator variables in the Replacement node. Change the role of these indicator variables to *input* in any subsequent modeling node before running the modeling node.

To see the impact of performing variable selection, connect the Variable Selection node to the Neural Network node. To do so,

1. Delete the connection between the Replacement node and the Neural Network node by selecting the line segment and pressing the Backspace or Delete key. Optionally, right-click on the line and select **Delete**.
2. Add a connection between the Variable Selection node and the Neural Network node.

Inspect the resulting process flow

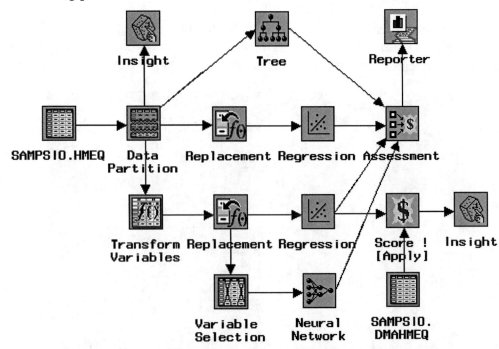

It is highly recommended that you perform some type of variable selection before proceeding in building Neural Network models. Neural Network models are very flexible, but are also very computationally intensive. Failure to reduce the number of input variables may result in

- an overfit model that does not perform well in practice
- a tremendous increase in the computational time that is necessary to fit a model
- computational difficulties in obtaining good parameter estimates.

Open the Neural Network node. The Variables tab is active.

Name	Status	Model Role	Measurement	Type	Format
BAD	use	target	binary	num	BEST12.
LOAN	don't use	rejected	interval	num	BEST12.
MORTDUE	don't use	rejected	interval	num	BEST12.
VALUE	don't use	rejected	interval	num	BEST12.
REASON	don't use	rejected	nominal	char	$7.
JOB	don't use	rejected	nominal	char	$7.
DEROG	use	input	interval	num	BEST12.
DELINQ	use	input	interval	num	BEST12.
CLAGE	use	input	interval	num	BEST12.
CLNO	don't use	rejected	interval	num	BEST12.

Observe that many of the variables have their Status set to *don't use*. Change the Status for M_VALUE, M_DEROG, and M_DELIN to *use* before proceeding. You could use the variable JOB instead of the grouped variable G_JOB by setting the Status for JOB to *use* and the Status for G_JOB to *don't use*, but that is not done here. Close the Neural Network node, and save changes when you are prompted. Then run the flow from the Assessment node and view the results when you are prompted.

Build a lift chart that compares all of the models by highlighting all of the rows and then selecting **Tools → Lift Chart**. The neural network shows some improvement in the first decile, although the stepwise regression model and decision tree still outperform the neural network.

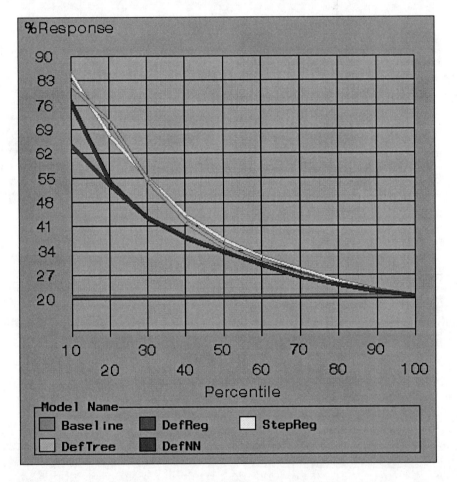

The output above is labeled by model names (select **Format → Model Name** from the lift chart window). You may need to maximize the window or resize the legend to see all of the model names.

As an exercise, consider revisiting the Variable Selection node and use the *Chi-square* criteria instead of the *R-square* criteria.

Chapter 4: Clustering Tools

4.1 Problem Formulation

Consider the following scenario. A baseball manager wants to identify players who are very similar with respect to several statistics of interest. Note that there is no response variable in this example. The manager simply wants to identify different groups of players. The manager wants to learn what differentiates players in one group from players in a different group.

The data is located in the DMABASE data set in the SAMPSIO library. A description of some key variables follows.

Name	Model Role	Measurement Level	Description
NAME	ID	Nominal	Player Name
TEAM	Rejected	Nominal	Team at the end of 1986
POSITION	Rejected	Nominal	Positions played in 1986
LEAGUE	Rejected	Binary	League at the end of 1986
DIVISION	Rejected	Binary	Division at the end of 1986
NO_ATBAT	Input	Interval	Times At Bat in 1986
NO_HITS	Input	Interval	Hits in 1986
NO_HOME	Input	Interval	Home Runs in 1986
NO_RUNS	Input	Interval	Runs in 1986
NO_RBI	Input	Interval	RBIs in 1986
NO_BB	Input	Interval	Walks in 1986
YR_MAJOR	Input	Interval	Years in the Major Leagues
CR_ATBAT	Input	Interval	Career Times At Bat
CR_HITS	Input	Interval	Career Hits
CR_HOME	Input	Interval	Career Home Runs
CR_RUNS	Input	Interval	Career Runs
CR_RBI	Input	Interval	Career RBIs
CR_BB	Input	Interval	Career Walks
NO_OUTS	Input	Interval	Put Outs in 1986
NO_ASSTS	Input	Interval	Assists in 1986
NO_ERROR	Input	Interval	Errors in 1986
SALARY	Rejected	Interval	1987 Salary in Thousands
LOGSALARY	Input	Interval	Log of 1987 Salary in Thousands

For this example, you will set the model role for TEAM, POSITION, LEAGUE, DIVISION, and SALARY to *rejected*. Set the model role for SALARY to *rejected* since this information is stored in LOGSALAR in the data set. No target variables are used in generating a Cluster Analysis or Self-organizing Map (SOM). If you want to identify groups based on a target variable, consider a predictive modeling technique and specify a categorical target.

4.2 *K*-means Clustering

Overview of Clustering Methods

Cluster analysis is often referred to as *supervised classification* since it attempts to predict group or class membership for a specific categorical response variable. Clustering, on the other hand, is referred to as *unsupervised classification* since it identifies groups or classes within the data based on all the input variables. These groups, or clusters, are assigned numbers; however, the cluster number cannot be used to evaluate the proximity between clusters. Self-organizing Maps (SOMs) attempt to create clusters and plot the resulting clusters on a map so that cluster proximity can be evaluated graphically, but that is not considered here.

Building the Initial Flow

Assemble the following diagram and connect the nodes as shown.

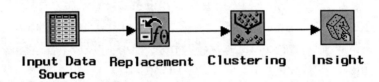

Setting Up the Input Data Source

Set up the initial Input Data Source as follows:
1. Open the Input Data Source node.
2. Select the DMABASE data set from the SAMPSIO library.
3. Set the model role for NAME to *id*, and set the model role for TEAM, POSITION, LEAGUE, DIVISION, and SALARY to *rejected*.
4. Explore the distributions and descriptive statistics as you want.

Select the **Interval Variables** tab and observe that the only variables that have missing values are SALARY and LOGSALAR. Select the **Class Variables** tab and observe that there are no missing values. None of the class variables have been included in this example. As an exercise, consider retracing the upcoming steps after using LEAGUE as an input variable.

5. Close the Input Data Source, saving changes when you are prompted.

Setting Up the Replacement Node

Although it is not always necessary to impute missing values, at times the amount of missing data may prevent the Cluster node from obtaining a cluster solution. The Clustering node needs some complete observations in order to generate the initial clusters. When the amount of missing data is too extreme, use the Replacement node to impute the missing values. This strategy was used for demonstration in this example, although it is not necessary in this case.

Setting Up the Clustering Node

1. Open the Clustering node.

The Variables tab is active when you open the Clustering node. *K*-means clustering is very sensitive to the scale of measurement of different inputs. Consequently, it is recommended that you use one of the standardization options if the data has not been standardized previously in the flow.

2. Select the **Std Dev.** radio button on the Variables tab.

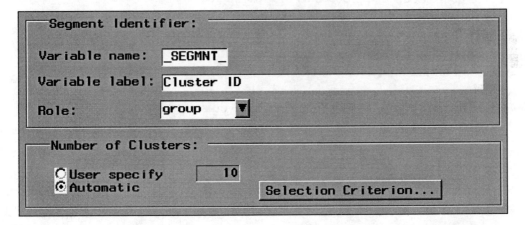

3. Select the Clusters tab.
4. Observe that the default method for choosing the number of clusters is *Automatic*.

By default, the Clustering node uses the Cubic Clustering Criterion (CCC) based on a sample of 2,000 observations to estimate the appropriate number of clusters. You can change the default sample size by selecting the **Data** tab and then selecting the **Preliminary Training and Profiles** tab. This example has only 322 observations, so all of the observations are used. The clustering algorithm determines a 40-cluster solution (by default). You can specify a different number of initial clusters by selecting the Selection Criterion button, but that is not done here. The algorithm then clusters the remaining clusters until all of the observations are in one cluster.

5. Close the Clustering node, saving changes when you are prompted.

Run the diagram from the Clustering node and view the results. The Partition tab in the results window is active.

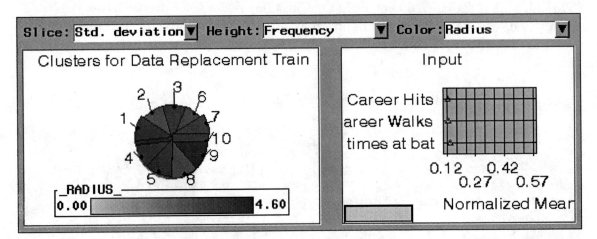

It is easy to see that the Clustering node chose a 10-cluster solution. The baseball manager feels that this many clusters may be hard to interpret and decides to limit the search to between 2 and 10 clusters. The algorithm now generates a 10-cluster solution initially, and then it clusters the clusters from the initial solution until all of the observations are in one cluster. These clusters are typically slightly different from those obtained earlier. Close the Clustering node results window.

To limit the number of clusters, proceed as follows:
1. Open the Clustering node.
2. Select the **Clusters** tab.
3. Select the **Selection Criterion...** button in the Number of Clusters section.
4. Type 10 for the Maximum Number of Clusters.
5. Select **OK**.
6. Close the Clustering node, saving changes when you are prompted.

Now rerun the flow from the Clustering node and view the results. The Clustering node returns a 3-cluster solution.

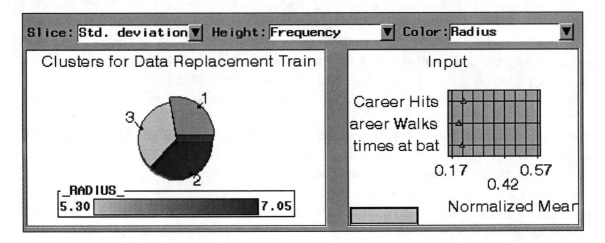

The manager decides to investigate this solution further. Select the **Tilt** icon (⊖) from the toolbar and tilt the 3-dimensional pie chart as shown below.

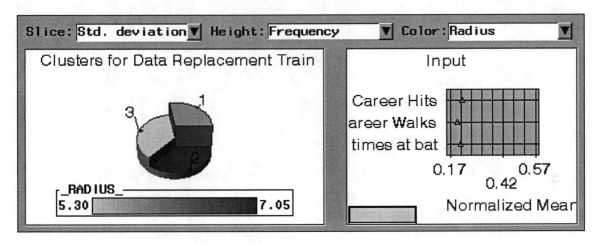

Inspect the chart in the left window of the Partition tab.

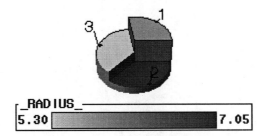

This chart summarizes three statistics of the three clusters. The options at the top of the Partition tab indicate that the

- size of the slice is proportional to the cluster standard deviation
- height of the slice is related to the number of observations in the cluster
- color indicates the radius (distance from the cluster center to the most remote observation in that cluster).

You can make some general observations that are based on this plot, including
- Cluster 1 contains the most cases, followed by cluster 3 and cluster 2.
- Cluster 3 has the smallest radius, while cluster 2 has the largest radius.

You can use the tilt and rotate tools to position the chart to evaluate wedge size, but that is not done here. Next, consider the right side of the window. It is often useful to maximize the window to see as much of the graph as possible.

Inspect the right side of the window. You may need to use the Move Graph tool (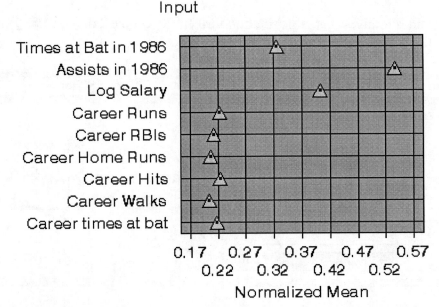) to see all of the variable labels.

Input

The right side of the window shows the Normalized Means for each input variable (mean divided by its standard deviation). Observe that not all of the variable labels are seen. Depending on your screen and window settings, you may see only some (or none) of these variables.

To see the other variables, select the **Scroll Data** tool (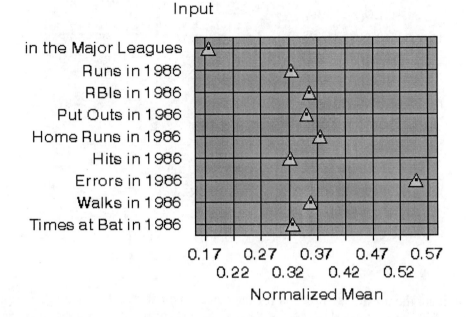) from the toolbar and drag in the plot. For example, scrolling to the top of the chart yields the following display. The label for the first variable is too long and is not completely visible in the window. Inspect the plot.

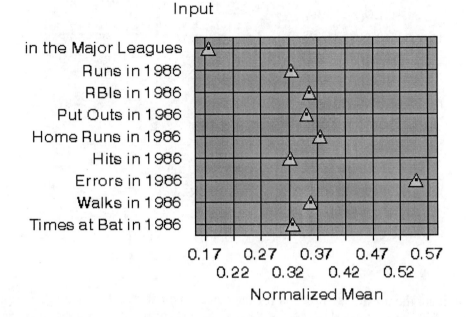

The Normalized Mean plot can be used to compare the overall normalized means with the normalized means in each cluster. To do so, proceed as follows:

1. Select the **Select Points** icon ( ) from the toolbar.
2. Select one of the clusters by clicking on the desired wedge in the three-dimensional pie chart. The example below shows the results for cluster 1.
3. Select the **Refresh Input Means Plot** icon ( ) from the toolbar.

After scrolling to the top, inspect the Normalized Mean Plot.

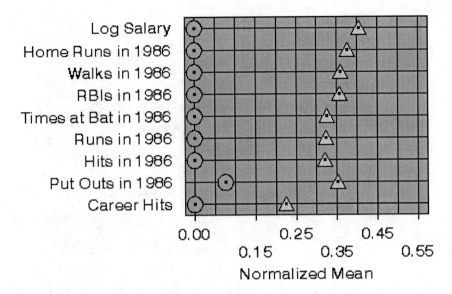

The circles indicate the normalized means for the selected cluster and the triangles represent the overall normalized means. Note that cluster 1 has values that are far below the average with respect to all of the variables that are shown above. If you scroll through the plot by using the Scroll Data tool, you will find that the players in cluster 1 are below the mean on all of the variables.

Consider the players in cluster 2. To do so, proceed as follows:

1. Select the **Select Points** icon ( ) from the toolbar.
2. Select cluster 2 in the three-dimensional pie chart.
3. Select the **Refresh Input Means Plot** icon ( ) from the toolbar.
4. Use the Scroll Data tool and scroll to the top of the output and inspect the resulting plot.

Inspect the plot for cluster 2.

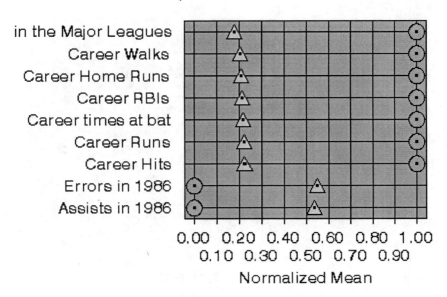

Cluster 2 contains players who have higher than average career stats and lower than average errors and assists in 1986. Scroll down to see the remaining variables.

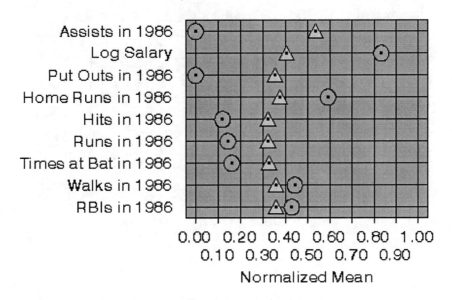

Cluster 2 players are also lower than average for their 1986 put outs, hits, runs, and times at bat. These players are higher on 1986 salary, home runs, walks, and RBIs.

Inspect the players in cluster 3 in a similar fashion.

Investigate the report for the cluster 3 players.

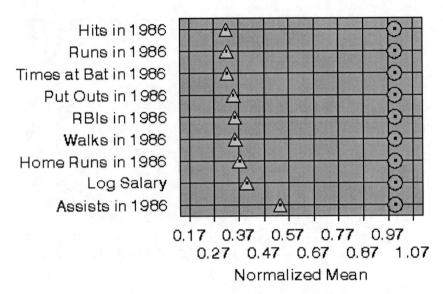

Cluster 3 players are much higher than average on their yearly statistics and salary.

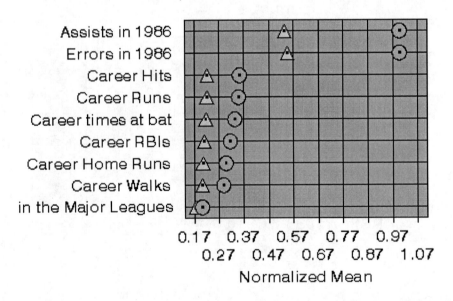

The career statistics for cluster 3 players are somewhat higher than average, and they have been in the major leagues an average number of years.

An admittedly oversimplified description for these clusters would suggest that

- cluster 1 players are young players with relatively little experience and relatively low lifetime and 1986 statistics.
- cluster 2 players are older players with relatively high lifetime statistics but somewhat average (or below average) 1986 statistics.
- cluster 3 players have a fair amount of experience and have somewhat average lifetime stats but high 1986 statistics.

Close the Clustering node when you have finished exploring the results.

The Insight node can also be used to compare the differences among the attributes of the prospects. Open the Insight node and select the option to use **Entire data set**. Close the Insight node, saving changes when you are prompted. Run the flow from the Insight node and view the results.

▶ 25		Nom		Nom	Int	Int
322		NAME	TEAM		NO_ATBAT	NO_HITS
■	1	Allanson, Andy	Cleveland		293	66
■	2	Ashby, Alan	Houston		315	81
■	3	Davis, Alan	Seattle		479	130
■	4	Dawson, Andre	Montreal		496	141
■	5	Galarraga, Andres	Montreal		321	87
■	6	Griffin, Alfredo	Oakland		594	169
■	7	Newman, Al	Montreal		185	37

All of the observations in the original data set are present, but the number of columns has increased from 23 to 25. Scroll to the right to identify the two new columns.

▶ 25		Int	Int	Int	Int	Int
322		NO_ERROR	SALARY	LOGSALAR	_SEGMNT_	DISTANCE
■	1	20	.	5.9272	1	3.1433942072
■	2	10	475.000	6.1633	1	2.7064870361
■	3	14	480.000	6.1738	3	3.0773462954
■	4	3	500.000	6.2146	3	3.0806907246
■	5	4	91.500	4.5163	1	3.0854258867
■	6	25	750.000	6.6201	3	4.3658691857

The column _SEGMNT_ identifies the cluster, and the column DISTANCE identifies the distance from each observation to its cluster mean.

Use the analytical tools within Insight to evaluate and compare the clusters. Begin by looking at the yearly statistics. The following steps represent one way to make these comparisons:

1. Change the measurement scale for _SEGMNT_ from interval (Int) to nominal (Nom) by clicking on the measurement scale (that is, **Int**) directly above the variable name, and then selecting **Nominal** from the pop-up menu.

▶ 25		Int	Int	Int	Nom	Int
322		NO_ERROR	SALARY	LOGSALAR	_SEGMNT_	DISTANCE
■	1	20	.	5.9272	1	3.1433942072

2. Select **Analyze → Box Plot/Mosaic Plot**.

3. Highlight **NO_ATBATS** through **NO_BB**. You can do so by dragging through the list or by selecting **NO_ATBATS** and then SHIFT-clicking on **NO_BB**.
4. Select **Y**.
5. Scroll to the bottom and select **_SEGMNT_**.
6. Select **X**.
7. Select **OK**.

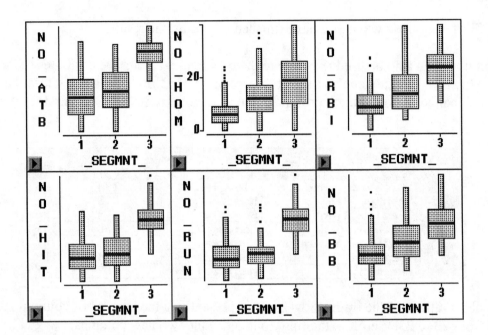

Cluster 3 is high on all of these statistics. Clusters 1 and 2 perform more similarly with respect to these statistics.

Investigate the career statistics as well by evaluating YR_MAJOR through CR_BB.

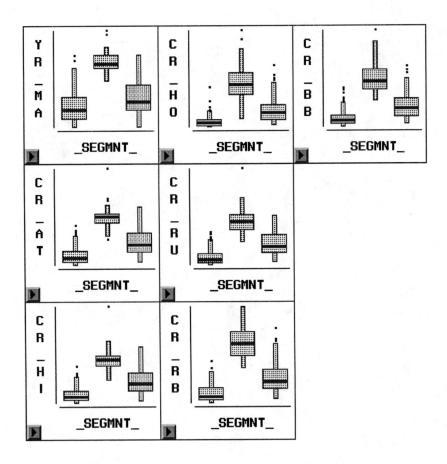

Observe that cluster 2 is high on most of these career statistics while clusters 1 and 3 are more similar.

Note that this type of plot works only for variables that have the same measurement level. The plots above are displayed for variables that are identified as interval variables (Int) in the Insight data table. If you try to specify both nominal and interval variables as Y when you invoke a Box Plot/Mosaic Plot, Insight will return an error. You must look at the nominal variables together and the interval variables together. You can have multiple plots open at the same time, however, so this does not pose a problem.

In addition, note that only a subset of the variables was used at one time. Insight sizes the plots based on the number of plots. Selecting too many variables results in the generation of many small plots, which may be difficult to read. While resizing individual graphs is easy, resizing all of them is more time-consuming, so it is best to look at specific subsets when you are plotting.

Generating several cluster solutions is fairly easy, but interpreting a particular cluster solution can be extremely challenging. It may be that no easy or useful cluster interpretation is possible. Since clusters naturally partition the population into mutually exclusive sets, they may provide some benefit even if a convenient interpretation is not readily available.

Chapter 5: Association Analysis

5.1 Problem Formulation

Consider the following scenario. A store seeks to examine its customer base and to understand which of its products tend to be purchased together. It has chosen to conduct a market-basket analysis of a sample of its customer base.

The ASSOCS data set lists the grocery products that are purchased by 1,001 customers. Twenty possible items are represented:

CODE	PRODUCT
apples	apples
artichok	artichokes
avocado	avocado
baguette	baguettes
bordeaux	wine
bourbon	bourbon
chicken	chicken
coke	cola
corned_b	corned beef
cracker	cracker
ham	ham
heineken	beer
herring	fish
ice_crea	ice cream
olives	olives
peppers	peppers
sardines	sardines
soda	soda water
steak	steak
turkey	turkey

Seven items were purchased by each of 1,001 customers, which yields 7,007 rows in the data set. Each row of the data set represents a customer-product combination. In most data sets, not all customers have the same number of products.

You may want to construct the flow for this chapter in a new diagram. To construct a new diagram, proceed as follows:
1. Select the **Diagrams** subtab from the left side of the Enterprise Miner window.
2. Select **File → New → Diagram**. Alternately, you can right-click in the portion of the window that displays the diagrams and select **New diagram**.
3. Edit the name of the new diagram if you want. For example, you may want to name the diagram Associations.

5.2 Understanding Association Results

Construct the following diagram.

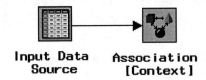

Input Data   Association
Source   [Context]

Specify the settings for the Input Data Source node.
1. Open the Input Data Source node.
2. Select the ASSOCS data set from the SAMPSIO library.
3. Set the Model Role for CUSTOMER to *id*.
4. Set the Model Role for PRODUCT to *target*.
5. Set the Model Role for TIME to *rejected*.
    Note: TIME is a variable that identifies the sequence in which the products were
    purchased. In this example, all of the products were purchased at the same time, so
    the order relates only to the order in which they are priced at the register. Association
    analysis where order is taken into account is known as Sequence analysis, although
    this type of analysis is not demonstrated here.
6. Close and save changes to the Input Data Source node.

Open the Association node. The Variables tab is active by default. Inspect the tab.

Name	Status	Model Role	Measurement	Type
CUSTOMER	use	id	interval	num
PRODUCT	use	target	nominal	char

Select the **General** tab. This tab enables you to modify the analysis mode and control
how many rules are generated.

Analysis mode: ⊙ By Context   ○ Association   ○ Sequences

┌─Minimum Transaction Frequency to Support Associations:─────────
│   ⊙ 5% of largest single item frequency
│   ○ Specify a count: [   ]

Maximum number of items in an association: [4   ]

Minimum confidence for rule generation: [10] %

Understanding Analysis Modes

Inspect the Analysis mode portion of this dialog box.

```
Analysis mode:      ⊙ By Context    ○ Association   ○ Sequences
```

The default analysis mode is By Context. This mode uses information that is specified in the input data source to determine the appropriate analysis. If the input data set contains
- an ID variable and a target variable, the node automatically performs an association analysis.
- a sequence variable that has a status of *use*, the node performs a sequence analysis. A sequence analysis takes into account the order in which the items are purchased in calculating the associations. A sequence analysis requires the specification of a variable whose model role is sequence. An association analysis ignores this ordering.

Other options include
- Minimum Transaction Frequency to Support Associations - specifies a minimum level of support to claim that items are associated (that is, occur together in the database). The default frequency is 5%.
- Maximum number of items in an association - determines the maximum size of the item set to be considered. For example, the default of four items indicates that up to 4-way associations are performed.
- Minimum confidence for rule generation - specifies the minimum confidence to generate a rule (Note: confidence is defined later). The default level is 10%. This option is unavailable if you are performing a sequence discovery.

Use the default Association settings. Close the Association node. Since you did not make any changes, you should not be prompted to save the changes. If you are prompted to save changes, select **No**. Run the diagram from the Association node and view the results.

The Rules tab is displayed first.

	Relations	Lift	Support(%)	Confidence(%)	Rule
1	2	1.25	36.56	61.00	heineken ==> cracker
2	2	1.25	36.56	75.00	cracker ==> heineken
3	2	1.11	26.07	43.50	heineken ==> baguette
4	2	1.11	26.07	66.58	baguette ==> heineken
5	2	1.35	25.67	42.83	heineken ==> soda
6	2	1.35	25.67	80.82	soda ==> heineken
7	2	1.11	25.57	52.67	hering ==> olives
8	2	1.11	25.57	54.12	olives ==> hering
9	2	1.38	25.17	82.62	artichok ==> heineken
10	2	1.38	25.17	42.00	heineken ==> artichok

The Rules tab contains information for each rule. Consider the rule A=>B in which A and B each represent one product, then observe the following:

- Support(%) for A=>B is the percentage of customers who have both A and B.
- Confidence(%) for A=>B is the percentage of customers who have A and who also have B.
- Lift of A=>B is a measure of strength of the association. If Lift=2 for the rule A=>B, then a customer having A is twice as likely to have B as a customer chosen at random.

Click on the Support(%) column with the right mouse button and select **Sort →
Descending**.

	Relations	Lift	Support(%)	Confidence(%)	Rule
1	2	1.25	36.56	75.00	cracker ==> heineken
2	2	1.25	36.56	61.00	heineken ==> cracker
3	2	1.11	26.07	66.58	baguette ==> heineken
4	2	1.11	26.07	43.50	heineken ==> baguette
5	2	1.35	25.67	42.83	heineken ==> soda
6	2	1.35	25.67	80.82	soda ==> heineken
7	2	1.11	25.57	54.12	olives ==> hering
8	2	1.11	25.57	52.67	hering ==> olives
9	2	1.38	25.17	82.62	artichok ==> heineken
10	2	1.38	25.17	42.00	heineken ==> artichok

Recall that Support(%) is the percentage of customers who have all the services that are involved in the rule. For example, 36.56% of the 1,001 customers purchased crackers and beer (rule 1), 25.57% purchased olives and herring (rule 7).

Consider the Confidence(%) column.

	Relations	Lift	Support(%)	Confidence(%)	Rule
1	2	1.25	36.56	75.00	cracker ==> heineken
2	2	1.25	36.56	61.00	heineken ==> cracker
3	2	1.11	26.07	66.58	baguette ==> heineken
4	2	1.11	26.07	43.50	heineken ==> baguette
5	2	1.35	25.67	42.83	heineken ==> soda
6	2	1.35	25.67	80.82	soda ==> heineken
7	2	1.11	25.57	54.12	olives ==> hering
8	2	1.11	25.57	52.67	hering ==> olives
9	2	1.38	25.17	82.62	artichok ==> heineken
10	2	1.38	25.17	42.00	heineken ==> artichok

Confidence(%) represents the percentage of customers who have the right-hand side (RHS) item among those who have the left-hand side (LHS) item. For example, of the customers who purchased crackers, 75% purchased beer (rule 1). Of the customers who purchased beer, however, only 61% purchased crackers (rule 2).

Lift, in the context of association rules, is the ratio of the confidence of a rule to the confidence of a rule, assuming the RHS was independent of the LHS. Consequently, lift is a measure of association between the LHS and RHS of the rule. Values that are greater than one represent positive correlation between the LHS and RHS. Values that are equal to one represent independence. Values that are less than one represent negative correlation between the LHS and RHS.

Click on the Lift column with the right mouse button and select **Sort → Descending**.

	Relations	Lift	Support(%)	Confidence(%)	Rule
1	4	5.67	8.99	71.43	peppers & avocado ==> sardines & apples
2	4	5.67	8.99	71.43	sardines & apples ==> peppers & avocado
3	4	5.64	11.59	82.86	ice_crea & chicken ==> sardines & coke
4	4	5.64	11.59	78.91	sardines & coke ==> ice_crea & chicken
5	4	5.57	9.59	66.21	ice_crea & bourbon ==> turkey & coke
6	4	5.57	9.59	80.67	turkey & coke ==> ice_crea & bourbon
7	4	5.53	11.59	83.45	coke & chicken ==> sardines & ice_crea
8	4	5.53	11.59	76.82	sardines & ice_crea ==> coke & chicken
9	4	5.48	9.09	72.22	peppers & avocado ==> sardines & baguette
10	4	5.48	9.09	68.94	sardines & baguette ==> peppers & avocado

The lift for rule 1 indicates that a customer who buys peppers and avocados is about 5.67 times as likely to purchase sardines and apples as a customer taken at random. The Support(%) for this rule, unfortunately, is very low (8.99%), indicating a relatively rare occurrence of the event where all four products are purchased together.

Your Turn

If you have comments or suggestions about *Data Mining Using Enterprise Miner™ Software: A Case Study Approach, First Edition*, please send them to us on a photocopy of this page or send us electronic mail.

For comments about this book, please return the photocopy to

SAS Institute
Publications Division
SAS Campus Drive
Cary, NC 27513

e-mail: yourturn@sas.com

For suggestions about the software, please return the photocopy to

SAS Institute
Technical Support Division
SAS Campus Drive
Cary, NC 27513

e-mail: suggest@sas.com

*Welcome * Bienvenue * Willkommen * Yohkoso * Bienvenido*

SAS® Institute Publishing Is Easy to Reach

Visit our Web page located at www.sas.com/pubs

You will find product and service details, including

- **sample chapters**
- **tables of contents**
- **author biographies**
- **book reviews**

Learn about

- **regional user-group conferences**
- **trade-show sites and dates**
- **authoring opportunities**
- **custom textbooks**

Explore all the services that SAS Institute Publishing has to offer!

Your Listserv Subscription Automatically Brings the News to You

Do you want to be among the first to learn about the latest books and services available from SAS Institute Publishing? Subscribe to our listserv **newdocnews-l** and, once each month, you will automatically receive a description of the newest books and which environments or operating systems and SAS release(s) that each book addresses.

To subscribe,

1. Send an e-mail message to **listserv@vm.sas.com.**

2. Leave the "Subject" line blank.

3. Use the following text for your message:

    subscribe NEWDOCNEWS-L *your-first-name your-last-name*

    For example: subscribe NEWDOCNEWS-L John Doe

Create Customized Textbooks Quickly, Easily, and Affordably

SelecText® offers instructors at U.S. colleges and universities a way to create custom textbooks for courses that teach students how to use SAS software.

For more information, see our Web page at **www.sas.com/selectext**, or contact our SelecText coordinators by sending e-mail to **selectext@sas.com**.

You're Invited to Publish with SAS Institute's User Publishing Program

If you enjoy writing about SAS software and how to use it, the User Publishing Program at SAS Institute offers a variety of publishing options. We are actively recruiting authors to publish books, articles, and sample code. Do you find the idea of writing a book or an article by yourself a little intimidating? Consider writing with a co-author. Keep in mind that you will receive complete editorial and publishing support, access to our users, technical advice and assistance, and competitive royalties. Please contact us for an author packet. E-mail us at **sasbbu@sas.com** or call 919-677-8000, then press 1-6479. See the SAS Institute Publishing Web page at **www.sas.com/pubs** for complete information.

See *Observations*®, Our Online Technical Journal

Feature articles from *Observations*®: *The Technical Journal for SAS*® *Software Users* are now available online at **www.sas.com/obs**. Take a look at what your fellow SAS software users and SAS Institute experts have to tell you. You may decide that you, too, have information to share. If you are interested in writing for *Observations*, send e-mail to **sasbbu@sas.com** or call 919-677-8000, then press 1-6479.

Book Discount Offered at SAS Public Training Courses!

When you attend one of our SAS Public Training Courses at any of our regional Training Centers in the U.S., you will receive a 15% discount on book orders that you place during the course. Take advantage of this offer at the next course you attend!

SAS Institute
SAS Campus Drive
Cary, NC 27513-2414
Fax 919-677-4444

E-mail: sasbook@sas.com
Web page: www.sas.com/pubs
To order books, call Fulfillment Services at 800-727-3228*
For other SAS Institute business, call 919-677-8000*

* Note: Customers outside the U.S. should contact their local SAS office.